Tales from the Riverside

Tales from the Riverside

Larry Landgraf

Fresh Ink Group
Guntersville

Tales from the Riverside

Copyright © 2018
by Larry Landgraf
All rights reserved

Fresh Ink Group
An Imprint of:
The Fresh Ink Group, LLC
Box 931
Guntersville, AL 35976
Email: info@FreshInkGroup.com
FreshInkGroup.com

Edition 1.0   2018

Book design by Ann E. Stewart
Cover photo by Larry Landgraf
Cover by Stephen Geez/FIG
Photos by Larry Landgraf, NOAA, and GoogleEarth

Except as permitted under the U.S. Copyright Act of 1976, no part of this publication may be reproduced, distributed, or transmitted in any form or by any means, or stored in a database or retrieval system, without prior written permission of the Fresh Ink Group, LLC.

All characters appearing in this work are from the author's honest and candid recollections.

BISAC Subject Headings:
BIO026000   BIOGRAPHY & AUTOBIOGRAPHY / Personal Memoirs
BIO002000   BIOGRAPHY & AUTOBIOGRAPHY / Cultural, Ethnic & Regional / General
BIO007000   BIOGRAPHY & AUTOBIOGRAPHY / Literary Figures

Library of Congress Control Number: 2018940782

ISBN-13: 978-1-947867-19-2 Papercover
ISBN-13: 978-1-947867-18-5 Hardcover
ISBN-13: 978-1-947867-20-8 Ebooks

Table of Contents

Prologue 1
Introduction 3
It Could Have Been Much Different 11
Mean Machine 13
Gardening and Fire Ants 15
You Always Need to Watch Your Step 18
City Gals and Fishing 20
Swimming in 40-Degree Weather 22
Catching Moccasins 24
Great Balls o' Fire 26
Swimming with Gators 29
Gars 'n' Gators 31
Gar Fishing 37
The Flats 40
Not Enough Water 44
Homer's Goat 47
Gambling is in My Blood 53
Mama Told Me 55
Mama's Recipes 58
You Are What You Eat! 67
Super Dogs 72
Sharing a Hole with a Snake 75
My Good Friend Bubba 77
Babies! 79
War in the Swamp 81

What's That in the Air Conditioner Condenser? 83
You Just Never Know…A Fishing Story!. 85
Before Today She Could Only Imagine the Excitement!. 86
A Leisurely Stroll Outside 88
Our Wild Sex Life 91
Peaceful Valley 93
Life is Great When It's Uneventful! 96
The Day My World Blew Up in My Face, Literally! 100
Dangers of the Deep. 113
Who's to Blame…Our Dying Estuary 115
That Son-of-a-bitch Harvey Almost Got the Best of Me 119
Aftermath: Harvey Lives On! 124
Smell the Roses! 131
Epilogue 135
My Swamp (poem) by Larry Landgraf 136
About Larry Landgraf 139

Prologue

I have been an author since 1986, when I wrote my first book, *Dangerous Waters*, which is now out of print. I wrote this book with enthusiasm and passion to try to save my first profession. I was only interested in saving my career, and did not plan to become an author.

I didn't write another book for twenty-six years. I wrote *How to Be a Smart SOB Like Me* in 2012, probably out of frustration, but again I wrote with enthusiasm and passion. Still, I did not plan to become an author, but the handwriting was on the wall—my second career had failed. But, I no longer needed the business.

In January 2015, I awoke from a dream and with a story in my head. I started writing, and before I knew it, I'd written another book, my first novel. I did not consider myself an author at this point, but something seemed to be pushing me in this direction.

I've since turned this first novel into my *Four Seasons Series*. Now that I'm working on book four of the series, I consider myself a bona fide author. Nothing was planned, but a little voice in the back of my head drove me to where I am today.

Introduction

Hi, my name is Larry Landgraf, and I'm a swamp dweller. All the stories in this book are true and as accurate as my memory allows. I have not tried to exaggerate the stories—the dangers of the swamp are extreme, and there is no need for exaggeration. I chose to live this lifestyle early on. I have no regrets and wouldn't have it any other way.

Why would I subject myself to this type of danger? Many of the stories contained in this book are not about the hazards, but rather are about the beauty of the swamp. By the time you finish the stories, you will understand that while there is great danger here, the swamp is also an abundant and beautiful place.

I first moved into the swamp in 1964 when I was sixteen, though I had been living in the area since birth. My mother re-married and moved to the Guadalupe River just across the river from my dad's property. I moved there with my mom and step-dad. That was when I officially became a swamp dweller.

One of the first things that showed me how dangerous this place was, wasn't a critter at all; it was flooding, and I got my first real taste of a major rise on the river in 1967. Hurricane Beulah was a huge, slow-moving storm that dumped torrential rains over much of central Texas in a week's time. The flood dealt out some severe damage.

I was just starting college in Victoria, Texas, and my first car, a Pontiac Bonneville, which was new to me that year, had water on the front seat when I crawled into it well before daylight that dreadful morning. The car started, to my surprise, and I headed to the highway where I could park on high ground. The Bonneville died as I backed up, but re-started and I headed for the low spot on the road leading to the highway. In the low spot, the car sputtered, and the water came all the way up to the windshield, but it kept going. I made it to high ground, opened the door, and water poured out. My car was okay. My mom's car and my step-dad's truck were not as lucky. Later that day, you couldn't see my mom's car parked in the front driveway. It was completely submerged.

I have become accustomed to the flooding by now. I have been through every flood here for the past fifty-four years. Three floods were categorized as 100-year floods, one as a 500-year flood, and I'm guessing maybe fifteen minor rises. When you live in a flood zone, water in the yard can be expected. You just hope there will never be a major flood, but I've gone through too many of those—more than I should have in my lifetime. I'm never happy when there is major flooding, but I do expect it to happen; just not so often.

Springtime and Fall flooding from warm and cold fronts are common, but hurricanes are also big contributors to high waters. I can't count the number of hurricanes and tropical storms I've lived through. I remember one in particular, which hit my home dead center with hundred-mile-per-hour winds. When the eye went over the house, we went outside and looked around. The sun came out and the wind was light. A short while later though, the wind came out of the opposite direction with a vengeance as the eye of the storm moved away.

During another hurricane, while I was home from college, I spent the night in a local tavern with some buddies and the owner. He closed the bar, and we played poker and drank beer all night while the storm with near hundred mile-per-hour winds raged outside. We played our game, and the back wall of the building swayed to-and-fro. After sunrise, we went out and drove around, as the wind had died down below fifty miles per hour. This was one of many hurricane parties I've attended.

Another danger I ran into when I first moved to the Guadalupe River was poison ivy. This wicked little plant grows wild here. Flooding does not affect the plant adversely, and during dry spells, there is always enough moisture in the ground that the plant grows like the wildest of weeds. If you've never had the burns and blisters the plant causes, it's hard to describe what it can do to you. The itch cannot be easily controlled even with modern medicines, and it will last at least a week or so even if doctored regularly.

It didn't take long to find out a lot of snakes live in a swamp. Mosquitos can get so thick, you can slap your hands together and kill dozens. Black river gnats will bite your scalp and drive you nuts in minutes. And bugs don't care whether they fly into your ears, up your nose, or into your mouth. If they crawl, they'll crawl up your britches and any other opening they can find in your clothing. There are sprays which can help, but insecticides will not always stop them, and you'll eat a few if you're not careful.

I have literally 'trampled' over snakes my entire life. I went out to our storage room at the back of our home one night. I was wearing jeans and shoes that particular time, and as I was searching for the light switch, I felt something hitting my leg. I looked down to see what it was. Turned out, I was standing on a coral snake!

Coral snakes are highly venomous, but their mouths are small. They have a difficult time biting you on large areas like your legs. They are more apt to strike a finger or toe. I was wearing shoes, so I was not in any real danger, but it's always a little spooky when you step on a venomous snake.

Coral snakes are similar to king snakes in color. They both have red, yellow, and black alternating bands. If the red bands touch the black ones, it's a king snake. If the red touches the yellow, it is poisonous and is a coral snake. As the saying goes 'red on yellow, kill a fellow; red on black, friend of Jack'.

One day while duck hunting, Cousin Steve's dog was barking under a large shrub. She had found a rattlesnake. Being the kids we were at the time, we wanted the snake for its hide. They make excellent hatbands.

I was squatting trying to get a good shot at the snake's head when my cousin walked around to my side of the bush. I moved over to give him some room, and he nearly stepped on a second rattlesnake where I was squatting. He jumped back and shot that snake. I'll never forget the look on Steve's face. He then took a stick and helped me get a shot at the head of the other rattler. We both got a hatband that day.

Another day, that same cousin and I were hunting dove. As we walked down a dirt road on the property, our eyes to the sky looking for birds, him walking down one trail and me on the other, we heard a rattlesnake. We turned around to see the snake coiled up in my cousin's path. Another hatband that day too.

I married after four years of college, and in 1971, I moved onto my dad's property directly across the river from where I had lived with my mother and step-dad. There, I officially began the first of three careers I would have during my lifetime; a commercial fisherman, the second as a general contractor, and the third, an author.

My wife and I lived there until 2008 when we divorced. The marriage produced three kids, but after 38 years, she just walked away. I kept the home I built with my own two hands, and that is where I currently reside.

In 2015, after six years commuting back and forth, first to Austin and then to San Antonio when Ellen moved there, I brought her to live in my swamp. Ellen and I had been dating for six years, and we now decided we wanted to spend the rest of our lives together. She was originally from New York City, moved to California, then to Austin for a new job. We met on a dating site while she lived there. I later helped her move to San Antonio.

Ellen had been visiting me about every other weekend, so she thought she knew what she was getting into, but visiting and living in a swamp are two different stories.

It just so happened that soon after she moved in, she got her first taste of flooding. The water rose to about a foot deep in the yard and was no big deal to me, but Ellen was quite concerned. I assured her everything would be fine and it was. There was no significant damage other than the inconvenience of water in your yard.

Ellen also got a better idea of how bad the mosquitos can get around here. She uses a lot of insecticide for the bugs. She also learned to watch where she was walking when she encountered her first water moccasin. It was lying in her path on the walk to her garden. These days, she has learned to accept the dangers, and I believe that now she loves the swamp almost as much as I do, especially the fishing.

We go out in the boat almost every week for fishing. We have only failed to bring dinner back one day in the several years I have been taking her out. There will be more stories that include Ellen.

An alligator we saw while fishing

My swamp is a dangerous place, and of course, there is the constant threat of flooding, but to Ellen and me, it is home. I wouldn't live anywhere else, and I will die here, which I very nearly did a time or two.

There are alligators up to fifteen feet long which can swallow a person, but these big boys (and girls) are rare to see. There are cougars and feral hogs which could cut and tear you to pieces, but like the larger alligators, these too are seldom seen, as they are mostly nocturnal. The day-to-day critters are always a threat like mosquitos, gnats, wasps, biting flies, spiders, and the ever-present snakes, but there are other dangers as well. There is mud that can swallow you up like quicksand, logs in the river which can rip the motor off your boat when you hit them, and treacherous flood waters.

An 8-foot alligator I got out of my pond

When it is hot and dry everywhere else, the swamp is green and alive. When it is cold, snowy, and desolate in most areas of the country, the swamp is warmer, sometimes greener, and usually alive with critters. To name a few: geese and ducks, fish in the river and streams, and deer and feral hogs—all excellent eating.

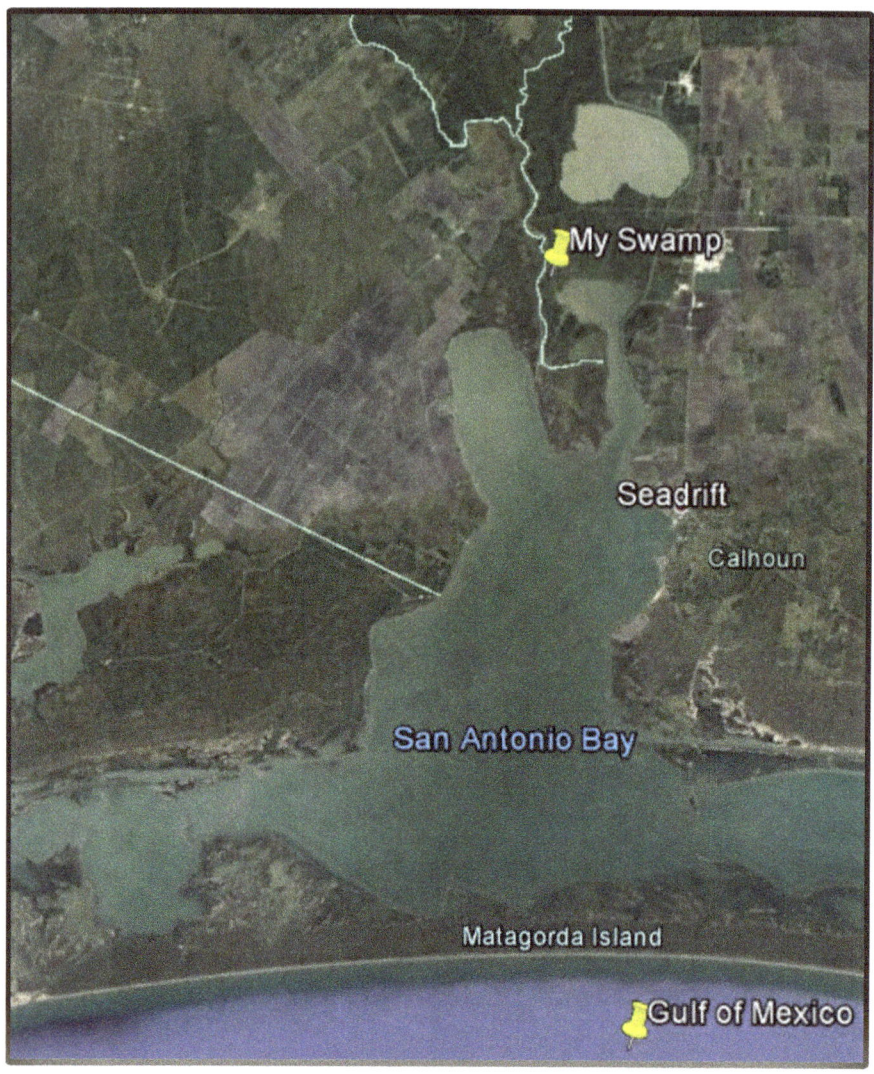

Map of the area

The relatively warmer waters of the nearby Gulf of Mexico, as well as the river, lakes, and streams of the Delta, help moderate the temperature. The humidity is often sky-high, and fog can roll in quickly, but I will take the milder temperatures any day. As an example, at this very instant, I went outside to check the thermometer. It is 10:22 a.m. on December 20th, the sky is clear and sunny, the wind is light, the temperature is 68°F, and it will rise to the upper 70's to near 80 degrees by late afternoon. What's not to like about that? It may change and likely will in a few days, but for the moment, the weather couldn't be more perfect. But as the saying goes in Texas, 'If you don't like the weather, just wait a little while'.

Some of the downsides to living here are that I usually need to mow the yard at least once even in December and January, and sometimes the mosquitos get quite bothersome even in times when there should be none. Also, occasionally and without warning, the weather can change drastically, the temperature dropping forty degrees, which is quite a shock. But much of the time, flowers still grow in the wintertime, fishing is often quite good, and there are usually many times when the weather is agreeable enough for a walk down our road.

I usually plant two gardens a year, or at least plant a portion of the space. The ground is super fertile and things grow very quickly.

I often have corn for Thanksgiving or Christmas depending upon when I plant, and some things will grow year-round like greens and herbs. I have one variety of peach tree that begins blooming in mid-January most years. It's quite nice to have such a long growing season, and when it gets above the hundred-degree mark inland, it seldom gets above ninety degrees in the swamp. Ninety-five here is a real scorcher.

A few things which are constantly on my mind these days, are safety, security, and resources. I will never run out of water, I am fairly isolated from the most dangerous animal on this planet, my fellow man, and there are more than enough resources on which to feed myself and family should I be forced to depend solely upon myself. I think about this often, about how many of you are entirely dependent, or nearly so, upon others for your very lives. Then I think about how competent these people are who provide you with all you need.

Think about this for a moment. How many things are provided for you which are vital to your survival? Water? Food? Heating? It may be easier to think about it in reverse. Name one or two things that you provide totally for yourself without the help of others. I'm not talking about buying stuff, I'm talking about producing things as in a garden or catching or killing your lunch; chopping your firewood, or having your own water well.

I'm guessing that the majority of you who read this book will not be able to come up with a single thing that you totally provide for yourself. This doesn't bother me, but if you actually think about it, it has to be pretty scary for you. What if suddenly you are thrust into circumstances where you must depend upon yourself for every need or you would die? What if suddenly your world is thrust into chaos like what happens in *Into Autumn,* book one of my *Four Seasons Series*? But you say, 'that cannot happen' or 'will not happen'. I'm just saying it can. I'm hoping it never happens, but what if it does? What are you going to do? My guess is you'll die from starvation along with millions of your neighbors, but also as likely, you'll be brutally murdered for your meager resources. Something to think about, isn't it?

But this book isn't about that. This book is about my life and the critters that play such a huge role in my daily activities. And remember, for every story I have written, there are dozens of other stories which have been omitted. You don't want to know, after all, about the hundreds of times the mosquitos have been unbearable.

I have added a year to the end of each story title to give you the approximate time the story occurred. Some of these stories happened a long time ago and the year may be approximate, but at least you'll be able to keep track of the timeline somewhat. At times a story will remind me of another story that may have happened at a different time, but at the same place. I've added a page break in these instances and included the new story as well.

That's enough of my rambling, which I tend to do from time to time now that I'm an author. Let's get you started on the stories. I've decided to open with an incident which happened back in 2013. I still shudder when I think about how easily I could have died.

It Could Have Been Much Different (2013)

When you live in a swamp, you expect to run into critters on a daily basis. One day, however, I literally ran into some nasty buggers I didn't expect. I knew they were around, but I had never seen them on my property and incidents with them were quite rare elsewhere. I never really expected that I'd run into these killers.

It was mid-summer, and I was doing some work in the pasture on my 65-year-old Farmall tractor. It was a not so hot day, but still quite warm and I was dressed accordingly. The T-shirt I was wearing left me highly exposed.

I was about 300 yards from the house when I drove my tractor into a hive, which was in a clump of saltgrass on the ground. Unlike honey bees, which in the wild live in trees, killer bees often make their nests on or near the ground. I drove the front wheels of the tractor over them, and hundreds of the little critters immediately swarmed over me. I threw the tractor into neutral and jumped off. I fell to the ground and the bees followed.

I got up quickly flailing my arms and took off running toward home. The bees followed in hot pursuit. The ground was uneven, and I fell twice more on the trek. I panted, and the falls drained my lungs and energy, but the relentless stings to my face, ears, neck, and arms forced me to get up. I ran the best I could. Each time I got up, I would glance at the house and safety. It seemed so far away.

The farther I ran, the fewer bees followed, but their numbers remained significantly more than I needed or wanted. When I finally reached the house, there were still a hundred or more bees chasing me.

I hurried through the door of the enclosed area of my back porch and slammed the door, then continued through the door at the other end of the porch hoping I could get away from the bees that still followed. I did elude the bees, but I had stings on my face, neck, and arms, so many so that I called Ellen and informed her that if I didn't call her back in 30 minutes, to call an ambulance. Ellen was 140 miles away in San Antonio.

I went inside and took two Advil and a Benadryl. I scraped off the stingers that I could find on my face and arms. I could see the marks where I had been stung. There were many—too many—but I was a tough guy, I thought. I wasn't allergic to bee stings, as I'd been stung many times before, but this time the sheer number of stings concerned me.

After thirty minutes, I had a slight headache, but no severe adverse reaction, so I called Ellen and told her I seemed to be okay. Then, I decided I should get my tractor back to the house. I had no bee suit, so I improvised. I donned my heavy winter overalls, made a hood out of a welding helmet and T-shirt, put on some gloves and boots, and taped up the seams.

When I reached the tractor, there were still a lot of bees around the still running and noisy machine, but they could not hurt me now. I drove the Farmall back to the house and parked it at the rear of my home. I went back onto the porch and took off my makeshift bee suit. I was soaked in sweat, as it was too warm a day for my heavy suit with no ventilation.

When I went back out to the tractor armed with insect killer, there were still a dozen or so bees flying around, and I noticed handfuls of dead bees around the exhaust manifold. The next morning, there were still a few bees around the tractor, but nothing to be concerned about. Persistent little turds! I went inside and got a can of flying insect killer and sprayed the few remaining bees without getting stung.

It's a good day when you survive a potentially deadly encounter, but in reality, it's just another day in the swamp. Find someone else to pick on, Mr. Grim Reaper! I'm not so easy to kill.

Mean Machine (2008)

Since I have already mentioned my 68-year-old tractor, I thought it would be fitting if I told you more about this badass machine. The Farmall Model M tractor was quite popular for many years, and there are still many of these tractors around and running. Years ago, I used to mow mesquite brush on the upland area of our property. I spent hours, days, and weeks mowing brush every year. All the wheels on the tractor are iron, so I never had flats, but the tractor continually broke down due to other reasons. The reason for the breakdowns was primarily due to the enormous task I was forcing the machine to tackle. This tractor had a heavy-duty mower deck on back and a push bar in front. It would literally cut up anything the tractor could push down. In all the years mowing, I only ran into one tree the Farmall could not push over.

    The day came when I no longer needed the tractor, and it sat parked untouched for about six years. One day, however, I decided I wanted to try to get the tractor running again. I got a friend to help me tow the tractor to my house two miles away. This was quite an ordeal. We first had to break the frozen pistons free in the engine due to years of it sitting idle. My friend pulled the tractor, and I let out the clutch with the tractor in gear to turn the engine over. It took a few tries, but I got the motor to turn. We towed it to my home with my truck.

    When we reached the house, I took the head off the engine and cleaned it up, ground the valves, changed all the ignition parts, reworked the starter, and repaired a few oil, water, and propane leaks. The tractor ran on propane. It was converted from gasoline to gas vapor many years before. I bought an old tractor of the same model for parts and the next thing I knew it was time to give it a try. After only a few attempts, the tractor started up, but new problems developed. I worked on the tractor off and on another couple of weeks and eventually got it where I could use the mean machine once again.

    I used the old tractor to clean up the property near my home. Once I got the land mowed, the load on the tractor was significantly less than what it had been for so many years. I used the tractor to mow about seven acres around my home for about twelve more years. It was a sad day last year, when I had to retire the old Farmall once more. There were too many problems with the old machine and it was no longer possible to keep it in good enough condition to mow my extended yard. I now have a new Farmall tractor to mow the pasture, if you can call a 50-plus-year-old tractor new. Well, it's new to me.

My old machine is now a yard ornament. I just can't seem to force myself to dispose of this once great machine. I spent more hours mowing brush than I can count on this antique tractor. These endless hours also make up a lot of time thinking about so many different things—the future, the past, dreams, failures, that last limb which slapped me in the face when I was too slow to duck . . . Better keep your mind on what you're doing Mr. Landgraf!

My yard ornament tractor

While I am on the subject of my old tractor, I'd like to share an incident while mowing pasture a long time ago that could have easily been the end of me. I was cutting brush when the driveshaft to the mower deck broke at one of the u-joints. This chunk of iron (part of the driveshaft) flew up and hit me in the back of the head.

I was deep in the brush and no one would have come to check on me until after dark if something had happened. But that's always been the deal when I've been working alone much of my life. Anyway, I saw stars when this chunk of steel hit me in the head, and I got a little woozy. I could have easily fallen off the tractor and into the turning blades of the mower. That would have been certain death.

Thinking about it now, a limb could have knocked me off the tractor many times. But there have been so many days, and I'm talking hundreds, maybe thousands, where I have been working alone, miles up or down the river or out deep in the pasture, or marsh, where no one knew exactly where I was. Even when I was home alone and the killer bees got after me, there was no one around. I could have lain outside in the pasture and died, and no one would have found me for a day or two, at least, even this close to home. So many things could have happened to hurt me or strand me where no one would ever find me again. That was much of my life, but I guess that's what also made me so tough. Facing danger head-on and enjoying it.

Gardening and Fire Ants (2015)

Fire ants are a fact of life in Texas and many other southern areas of the country. I have been bitten more times than I can count, and usually a dozen or two bites at a time. They sting for a little bit, then they itch for a while, and the next day they are just another spot on my hands or feet. I accept the fact that I am going to get bitten on a regular basis, and they do not bother me long. I have toughened up to their bites. And their poison only makes me tougher the next time they get hold of me.

Now Ellen, on the other hand, is a city gal. She has never had so many critters trying to hurt her. I am tough meat to most critters, but Ellen is a tender target for most. Not only the fire ants, but mosquitos, biting flies, wasps, and most other small biting insects that are so numerous in the swamp, are a constant concern for Ellen. She is soft and sweet, and I even like to take a nibble on her from time to time myself.

A few days before our trip to Florida and then on to Costa Rica, Ellen was working in her garden. We have separate gardens. I gave her my small plot, which is plenty big enough for what she wants to grow, and I made a much larger garden for myself for what I want to produce. I grow the things which take more room like potatoes, corn, peanuts, beets, and melons, which happen to be the garden things I like most.

Anyway, Ellen was working in her garden, and some fire ants decided to make a nest in her bag of mulch. She was spreading the mulch around some of her plants and before she knew it, the ants were all over her hands. They bit her badly on both. That's probably the worst place to get bitten by fire ants. First of all, you use your hands constantly. Next, the bites tend to make the hands swell more than other places on your body, and they tend to heal up the slowest.

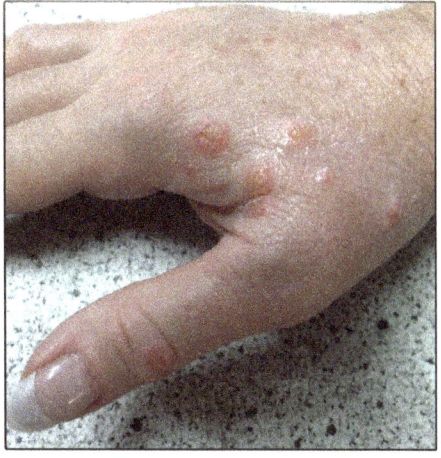

Ellen's hand with a few fire ant bites

Ellen's hands, especially her left one, puffed up like a balloon. She is left-handed like me, and this made the bites more debilitating for her. She doctored them for several days, and I could feel her pain, but there was nothing I could do.

They were quite painful for two days, then just uncomfortable for a few days more. They were then unsightly for days after that, but she used some makeup to cover up the blemishes. We headed for Florida to visit her dad and stepmother, and the wounds healed up nicely while there. By the time we headed for Costa Rica, she was mostly over the ordeal. Another lesson learned by my sweet little city slicker.

Ellen and I are from two different worlds. We get along splendidly and are a good match for each other. I could not live in the city, but Ellen lived on a farm for a few years and loves the country. I'm glad she decided to move to my swamp, but the adjustment for this city gal to the wildlife may take her a lifetime to get accustomed to. She will toughen up some over time, but I like the fact that she is soft and tender. I'm glad she's here. She is happy here too. I do my best to make certain of that. Taking her fishing on a regular basis is probably one of the biggest things I do to keep a smile on her face.

I'm going to stick in another quick story about Ellen, but this one is more recent than the one above. Ellen got a kick out of this one, which is why it is included.

We went fishing early this morning downstream from the house. We went to one of our favorite spots, which has been producing good fish lately, and we did well there again this morning. This was the first spot we wanted to fish, and we passed up several other favorite spots to get there.

After we caught several, we worked our way back upstream, stopping at other places we knew would be good. Another boat was parked in one of our very favorite spots, so we parked about fifty yards downstream from them. Two men in the other boat were yakking away and making all kinds of noise. They weren't catching any fish that we could see.

Ellen and I started catching fish as soon as we got the boat tied up. We were quiet except for the noise we made hauling the fish in. After we had caught at least six good fish, the men in the other boat cranked up their motor and left.

The men had to be talking about us and wondering how we were catching so many fish. I think that's why Ellen thought this would be a good story for the book. It gave her a good laugh anyway.

I'm sure they caught some fish somewhere, but as much noise as they were making, I wouldn't count on it. Noise does scare the bigger fish, and usually it is better if you're quiet as possible. Good bait, which we always have, and good technique is also a plus. Being an ex-commercial fisherman helps me, and I try to teach Ellen as much as I can.

We ended up with seventeen fish this morning. Ellen caught about half of them, and maybe one or two more than I did. Doesn't really matter. We both enjoyed our lunch equally, which consisted of catfish, Lars's Pickled Beets, and garlic bread. Ellen makes the best tartar sauce for the fish. I've gotta give her kudos for that.

Morning catch of catfish (already gutted and skinned)

You Always Need to Watch Your Step (2014)

One night long ago, after opening some boxes from items I had ordered online, I decided to take the empty containers out to the porch. I would dispose of them the following day. With the boxes in one hand, I flipped on the light switch to the porch and opened the door. I was barefoot and wearing shorts, as always, and as I went ahead through the opening and started to take my first step onto the rug just outside the door, I caught some movement out of the corner of my eye. The movement was on the rug where I was about to step. I stepped over this area and onto the bare wood just out past the carpet.

After I made that first long step, I turned to see what I had caught a glimpse of. To my surprise, there was a three-foot-long rattlesnake stretched out on the rug exactly where I was about to put my foot. After I made it past the reptile, it slithered off to a corner a few feet away. It had no way out except through me.

The snake coiled up, and we stared back at each other. I grabbed a mop to hold the snake down and yelled at Ellen. She found a crowbar in the garage for me to use to kill the snake. I maneuvered the critter, so that I could find its head. I held the rattler down with the mop and mashed his head in, killing him instantly.

I have seen rattlesnakes in the swamp before, but they are rare here. They like drier areas. Though the drought here is not nearly as bad as most areas of the state, it is still dry in the river bottom. Maybe there will be more rattlesnakes in my future. I will need to keep my eyes open. You just never know where they are going to show up—maybe at your doorstep one night!

After killing the snake, my next thought was a hatband. The rattler was long enough and very pretty colored with its signature diamondback pattern. I had often made hatbands and adorned my straw hats with them when I was a teenager. I immediately skinned the critter, tacked it to a board, and salted the hide for the night. I would deal with it further the next day.

The following morning, I scraped the skin to remove fat and excess tissue, salted it well, and placed it in the sun to cure. I repeated this process for several days, then cut the dried skin off the board. It was ready for the hat, but I had no straw hat. I remedied this problem the next time I went into town.

New cowboy hat with diamondback rattlesnake hatband

City Gals and Fishing (2015)

This morning, it was time to take Ellen fishing again. We loaded up the boat and headed down the river to see if we could once again catch dinner. Of all the trips we made in 2016 and 2017, we only failed to bring dinner home once. We went almost weekly, so this was a remarkable feat in itself.

I've tried to teach Ellen how to fish, and she does very well, but I usually catch the most fish, though this is not always the case for some strange reason. I'm the most experienced, so I should catch the most fish, right? While I continue to show her that my way is best, she continues to do a few things her way, but that's okay too. As long as she's happy, right? That's my thinking. After all, I used to be a commercial fisherman and have caught enough fish to last a lifetime. Ellen, on the other hand, has never had the opportunity to fish like she does now and insists we go often. For her happiness, that's fine with me. Besides, fresh catfish is my favorite fish to eat.

Some of the things Ellen does to my dismay is that she never thinks there are fish under the boat. She will cast her line at times some distance from the boat, and often upstream, which is also a no-no. There are a lot of trees everywhere up and down our river, and as such, these trees die on a regular basis and are scattered along the bottom. If you cast upstream, the line will drift down current and the chances are high for it getting hung up on a log. The same is true the farther you cast away from the boat. For this reason, over the past couple of months alone, Ellen has lost her tackle to snags at least a dozen or more times. Over the same period of time, I am still using the same sinker and hook I was using two months ago. She sees, but she refuses to adopt my method.

The last time we were fishing, I pointed to a spot where I knew a fish would be. I wanted her to catch all the fish that day. She did catch a fish where I told her there would be one, but I caught a bigger one straight down under the boat. She never said a word, but I did see the smirk.

It's been a couple of years or so since Ellen's first fishing trip. This morning she and I went out in the boat again. Ellen doesn't lose as much tackle these days, but still, more than I do. She is much better at re-doing her line now, which is one positive thing.

I almost never cast more than twenty feet or so from the boat. This morning I caught the first four keeper catfish before Ellen caught her first one, period. She blamed the seating positions, but fortunately, she started catching a few. In the end, she caught nearly as many as I did, and for a while, she had landed the biggest. As luck would have it, I broke her record. She didn't complain though, because we both caught several very nice fish.

I have absolutely nothing to criticize about Ellen's fishing anymore. She takes care of her tackle, baits her line like a pro, and takes the hooks out and puts the fish in the cooler. I still help her with snags from time to time and getting a hook out, which the fish swallowed, but I have no problem with that. It seems Ellen learns fishing skills slowly, but it is quite complicated, and I've been fishing and processing the things all my life. I could do it all blindfolded. And so what if it takes her a little longer to learn? She is improving daily, and she's doing very well now.

She's learning how to process the fish exactly as I do, so I really have nothing to nit-pick about, and I am not complaining in this story if it may sound that way. I'm, after all, a 'guy', and to us guys, things don't always sound like we mean them to sound to women. Enough said on that subject.

City gals can learn. Before long, she'll probably be telling me I'm doing a few things wrong myself . . . not! Probably should have edited this out. What do you think?

Swimming in 40-Degree Weather (1963)

Let's head way back to the sixties for a few earlier stories before I get too old and forget them. One of the reasons I can do so many things today is that I have been learning by doing stuff all my life. I learned from my mistakes, and I learned by watching grownups. The key is to be learning constantly. You sit on your butt doing nothing, and you're going to grow up fat and lazy. I may sit on my butt a bit more as an author, and over time it may spread a bit wider, but you can never honestly call me lazy. One thing you can call me, though, is a long-winded writer who strays often. If you're going to be sitting on your butt, you may as well be reading a book—learning something along the way. Now, let me see if I can locate the brain cells holding the next story.

Ah, here it is.

Cousin Steve and I were around fifteen years old. It was the fall of the year, and goose and duck season was open. Most weekends we spent in the marsh hunting. We tromped around in the mud, muck, and saltgrass for the elusive winged creatures.

One such weekend, Steve and I were taking a rest along the slough which ran through the swamp. This was a fly-way for ducks, but that particular day the ducks were few and far between.

I think Cousin Steve had already bagged a couple of birds, but I was still empty-handed. Luckily, I got my turn soon enough. A single duck came our way, and I got a good hit, but the thing fell dead on the far side of the slough.

Having been taught very well by my mom and dad not to waste food, there was only one thing to do. Though the temperature was in the mid-40's, I had to cross the waterway and retrieve the duck. Hypothermia was also a consideration. I needed to keep my clothes dry, so I stripped down to my tightie-whities.

The water was only about two feet deep, but the mud was bottomless. I had to be very careful not to get stuck in the mud banks of the ditch. I scooted across the slough as fast as possible. Once I retrieved the duck, I had to do it again to get back to Steve.

By this time, I was shaking severely as I dressed, and my teeth chattered for some time, but the dry clothes, though a bit muddy on the inside, warmed me up quickly once we resumed our trip across the swamp.

As I recall, I only had to do this on that one day. Another lesson learned the hard way. If you are going to have a difficult time retrieving the duck, don't shoot. Let it go. There will be another along, and if not, there will be another day.

Have you ever wondered what makes swamp people so tough? Well, it's stuff exactly like this. Stuff we have been doing all our lives—learning new things through making errors, avoiding mistakes the next time, but always finding new challenges to be met and overcome. So, the next time you meet a country guy or gal in the city who looks a little out of place, respect that he may look like a square peg in a round hole in the city, but he's learning. He knows to keep his eyes and ears open, and he will make it just fine in the urban setting. In the reverse though, you wouldn't survive long in his world, especially if his world happened to be a swamp.

Catching Moccasins (1962)

Smokey Creek, as it was named later in our lives after Cousin Steve's dad, ran through the upland section of our property and emptied into the swamp. My uncle worked at a carbon black plant near Rockport, Texas. The plant was always shrouded in a cloud of smoke. My uncle got the nickname 'Smokey' because he always came home a smoky gray color.

Back to the creek, at times you could step across it in places, while after very heavy rains, I've seen it raging 200-feet wide and 40-feet deep into Smokey River. This creek was a constant source of fun and adventures for Cousin Steve and me.

At times, we fished for blue crab, which would come up into the creek, catfish in the lower section where the creek was wider and deeper, crawfish in the shallow ponds, and of course the easiest to catch, perch in some of the deeper sections of the stream.

The major hazard of fishing in this creek was moccasins. This was one of the four venomous snakes found on the property. They are also called water moccasins. It's the same snake. They were primarily limited to areas around the creek, and we always needed to keep an eye out for these dangerous critters.

Occasionally, when we fished for perch, these venomous reptiles would try to bite the fish we had caught and were keeping in the water on a stringer. The perch on the stringer would splash around in the water and attract the snakes, but we learned quickly how to deal with these pesky reptiles. We didn't care if they were poisonous and could hurt or kill us. They were a problem, and we dealt with them as we saw fit.

We cut a length of our fishing line to make a snare in one end. We'd lay the dry fishing line, which would float on the water, then dangle our perch on the stringer inside the loop in the twine. When the snake approached our fish, we lowered the perch deeper into the water, so the snake would have to submerge to get to the fish. When it did, we raised the fish up through the loop, and the snake followed. A quick yank on the twine tightened the snare tight around the snake, and he couldn't get away.

We had to be very careful with the snake thrashing around to keep from getting bitten. We tied the twine to a limb and let the snake dangle to death.

Usually, by this time, the fish were scared enough that we could no longer catch any more and we went to another spot to fish or just went home if we had caught enough.

It was a dangerous little game, but we were careful, and continued to learn valuable lessons that would protect us later in life. If you are a grownup with teenage kids, imagine how you would feel if you knew your kids were doing some of the things we did every day. I doubt our moms and dads ever knew what kind of dangers we were getting into. If they did, they didn't talk about them and neither did we. We were just happy to be home and alive, and the next day the danger was forgotten. A new day, a new danger, and a new lesson to learn.

Great Balls o' Fire (1960)

I added this story at the request of my best friend, Robert C. I would not have shared this story as it is quite embarrassing, but Robert thought it was hilarious and should definitely be included in the book.

After the last couple of stories and a few more later in this book, you're learning that I spent a lot of time outside and with little protection from the critters. As a result, I spent a lot of time carrying chiggers around from the time I was ten up to fifteen. Chiggers are microscopic bugs that burrow into your skin. About two and a half million can fit on a single page of this book. It only takes a dozen to cause extreme pain and misery for a young kid.

After I got a little older, I learned to fight the critters more efficiently, and they bothered me less. For several years, however, they were the major misery in my life.

My parents divorced when I was in the fifth grade, so my sisters, my mother, and I moved to the nearby city of Port Lavaca. I was ripped away from the country living I loved, so I became a city dweller. On many weekends though, I spent time with Cousin Steve.

My mother divorced my dad because of his drunken behavior. This problem didn't go away until well after the split-up, maybe five years or more, and that is the reason I spent most of my time with Steve when I was supposed to be visiting my dad.

Steve and I ran wild in the pastures we had grown up on. Many weekends for several years, I would get a moderate to severe case of chiggers. You can't see them, and don't usually know you have them, until a day or so after you get the infestation.

I missed many Monday morning school days due to chiggers. The little critters are on the weeds and get on your clothing. They crawl up your legs and arms when you are out in the pasture. When they get to a spot where there is a constriction in your clothing, they burrow in. This is at the ankles, behind the knees, inside your arms at the elbow and shoulder, and a few make it around the waist. There are always some that make it to the groin area.

These little chiggers love the soft and tender areas of the groin. They have no shame in burrowing into your scrotum or penis. Then the itching and torture begin. I have tried every remedy known to man to stop the itching and get some relief. I'm going to share some of the more exotic remedies with you. Some worked better than others, while a few were quite painful. But the itch was horrendous. The more chiggers you get, the more agonizing the itch. Usually, a dozen was sufficient to be considered major torture, and often I had much more than that.

An early remedy as proposed by my mother was calamine lotion. It helped, but didn't work well or fast enough for me. Then I tried my own methods. Scratching open the surface of the insect bite and doctoring with full-strength bleach worked well, but wasn't perfect, so I continued my search for something better.

Campho-Phenique® is a good home remedy for many skin irritations and cuts, and it worked well on chiggers, but it took days to kill the little buggers and stop the itching. I learned that burning the bite area slowly with a cigarette would kill the insect and stop most of the itching, but it was quite painful for the few minutes of slow burning it took to kill the insect. It scabbed over and left a mark for a while, too. In addition, this is not something I wanted to do on my penis, though I was brave enough to do it on my scrotum, as this was always the site of the worst itch.

One day I discovered some Bengay® analgesic cream in my grandmother's medicine cabinet. After the divorce, my dad moved in with his mother for their mutual benefit, so when I stayed with my dad, I was actually staying with my grandmother. I had a good dose of chiggers that day and spread a generous amount of the cream on my scrotum. It didn't seem to do much at first other than make my eyes tear from the fumes. It wasn't long, however, until the cream kicked in and my balls were afire. Damn, they were roasting!

That day I learned a little something about analgesic creams. They penetrate the skin, and no amount of soap or water can get them out. You can get the cream off, but what's in the skin stays in the skin. I danced a jig you wouldn't believe unless you saw it, while at the same time trying to get that stuff off and cool the genitals. I think maybe I learned a few new obscenities that day.

After about thirty minutes, the effects of the analgesic cream began to wear off. I was certainly glad of that. This wasn't the first lesson I learned in my life, and it surely wouldn't be the last, but I learned this one well. What's worse was the Bengay® didn't even seem to faze the chiggers. Took my mind off them for about thirty minutes, but it wasn't worth it.

Swimming with Gators (1964)

When Cousin Steve and I were about sixteen, my dad and uncle, Steve's dad, had their own jobs, but were also partners in ranching and a few other local enterprises. The ranch consisted of about 850 acres in two sections. The major piece was upland stretching into the swamp to the Guadalupe River where I live today. The other smaller section was entirely in the swamp, downstream from where I live, close to the bay. This was the best place for duck hunting.

As the ranch was fairly large, there were always fences to repair or rebuild. One section that needed rebuilding ran across the creek through the property where it flowed into the swamp. The creek was about fifty feet across in this spot.

My uncle and dad drove Steve and me to the creek where the fencing needed to be strung. The first thing Steve and I noticed was that an alligator made the area his home. We pointed that out to our dads, but they didn't seem to think the critter was a problem and the fence work needed to be done regardless. "He's only about six feet long," my dad said. "He won't bother you." There were worse things to be concerned about in the water I guess, such as moccasins.

My dad and uncle used Cousin Steve and me often for manual labor, and much of this work was fence repairs around the property. We would have rather played, but they insisted we help. We were growing stronger due to their many chores, but we were also learning more about the farm and taking care of the hundred plus head of cattle our parents raised. Our dads had a plan. If we were to run the ranch later in life, we needed to learn the processes now.

My dad, uncle, Steve, and I stood surveying the creek that the fencing needed to cross. The distance was about 50 feet, and though the weather was cool, it wasn't cold enough to keep us out of the water according to our dads. We complained a little, but the elders knew how often we'd been in much colder water.

The alligator was at least a foot longer than we were tall, but our dads kept assuring us we'd be safe, so we slithered into the water with the end of the wire. The water was only about four-feet deep in the center, so we didn't have a problem pulling the wire across. We kept an eye on the gator, but it didn't seem to be interested in us. He did keep his eyes focused on us, but kept his distance.

We made two runs across the creek with a strand of wire each time and securely attached it to the post at the far edge. While Cousin Steve and I dried off and changed clothes, my dad and uncle secured the wires to the fence post on this side of the creek. They figured two strands of wire would deter the cattle from getting into the neighbor's pasture.

That was the first time I swam with alligators. If the gator had been a little bigger, my dad or uncle would have killed it. They are quite good eating, and when they get over eight feet in length, they are dangerous, not only to kids, but to cattle. They wouldn't tackle a grown cow, but many a calf has been killed in the swamp by large alligators. This is a fact.

Gars 'n' Gators (2013)

Most rivers here in the south have alligators and gar-fish. My river is no different. We have three species of gar—spotted, needlenose, and the big boy, alligator gar. I heard that someone caught an eight-foot alligator gar not long ago, upstream from here. They said it weighed 189 pounds. These big boys can hurt you just like an alligator. The only difference is they can't chase you on dry land because of the lack of legs. They can see well out of the water, and if you get too close, they will try to bite. If you happen to be in the water with a big one, they don't need legs.

Alligator gar

Needlenose gar are scarce, but they are around. They do not get as large as the more populous alligator gar, but they do get up to five or six feet. While they're not as big as the big boys, they are still damn big and can hurt you. Spotted gar are small and do not get much longer than three feet. There are quite a few of these.

Gar are survivors because of primarily one reason; they have gills to breathe underwater, and they also have lungs to breathe air when there is little or no oxygen in the water. They can live in stagnant pools.

All gar are decent eating if you cook them right. I don't care for them much, but I've eaten a few. The tough part is peeling the slimy and tough scaly armor off the critter. Their scales are connected with heavy cartilage. It bends yet does not come apart as scales on most other fish. With the proper technique, which I have, I don't have a problem cleaning them.

There are too many alligators around here these days, but that is just my opinion. They are good eating, but I don't care for them either. I have and will eat them, but there are better things to eat in this river—catfish. Killing alligators is a regular event around the house though. I don't like to kill them because I don't care to process them, but it must be done.

I tried to raise mallard ducks for several years, but alligators got most of them. I shot one gator with one of my ducks in its mouth. That was a sad day. The gator sank as they will do when you shoot them, but I took a photo of it with the duck still in its mouth a few days later when they bloated and floated to the surface.

Dead alligator with a pet duck in its mouth

We have blue crabs in the river in the late summer and early fall. They come up from the bay to grow up. Gar make good crab bait for use in our crab traps. Ellen likes to catch gar, and this works out great for me because we both love to eat crabs. Gar are more easily caught at night under a light. A couple of nights this past week, Ellen kept me up until after midnight. I need my beauty sleep, lol. The crabs are worth it though. In addition to a few gar, she also caught two alligators. I'll eat the crabs. Maybe we'll serve the gator up to friends and neighbors.

As it turned out, Ellen found a recipe for alligator that I love. Just marinate in buttermilk overnight, then drain, add some Louisiana hot sauce, roll in flour, and deep-fry or skillet fry if you don't have a deep-fryer. Tastes just like chicken . . . lol. Not really, but it does taste like chicken-fried pork. Now all you've gotta do is get your hands on an alligator tail and give it a try.

Make sure it's fresh though. Most things these days are so over-processed that the vast majority of people have no idea what many things even taste like. Take shrimp, fish, and oysters for example. We eat them fresh out of the water and process them ourselves. I've eaten fresh oysters in Las Vegas, and they have virtually no taste compared to the oysters I shuck and eat while they're still alive.

How many of you shuddered just then? Yes, live oysters are the best. It's good to chase them with some whisky though, to kill bacteria, which all oysters have when caught. I've never gotten ill from oysters I've shucked and eaten, but I did once with oysters I purchased. Getting sick on oysters is not something I'd recommend for anyone.

The title of this story is 'Gars and Gators', but I've gotten so far off the subject you're going to be calling me 'ramblin' man'. I do get sidetracked, but there wasn't anything else I wanted to say about gar. I'm sure there'll be more bits and pieces about them in other areas of the book.

Before I get away from this chapter, I'd like to mention a large species of shrimp that lives in the river here. I call them simply 'freshwater shrimp'. There is one more species that I call 'grass shrimp' but this species gets no more than an inch and a half long. I don't know their real names. Maybe I'll look them up one day . . . but not now.

The 'freshwater shrimp' grow to over eighteen inches long if you count the pincers. They are rare to catch, but they are quite good eating when I do catch one.

Freshwater shrimp

Since I did mention crabs up above, let me throw in a few more photos of those. Crabs usually come into the bays from the Gulf of Mexico in the spring. They need fresh water to grow up, and when they get into the river and bayous around here, they do grow quite large.

A dry summer and fall will produce quite large crabs. If we get too much fresh water and strong currents, the crabs are washed back out into the bay and are not easily accessible from my home. But much of the time, when the crabs are around, I can catch all I want in my backyard. How convenient and so tasty.

Blue crabs

Large blue crab

Crabs ready for cooking

Gar Fishing (2018)

When I got Tales from the Riverside *back from my proofreader, she said she loved the book. Then she added it would have been nice if there was at least one story from Ellen—get her perspective on what it's like living in my swamp. I had to twist her arm a little, but she finally conceded. This is her story.*

One of my very favorite things to do at the river is gar fishing. Larry taught me how. We use gar as crab bait, and Larry does love his crabs ☺, so he encourages me. I fish for gar late at night, and it's truly a magical experience. The ones I usually catch are spotted gar, a lovely yellowish spotted fish. Not too big. The biggest one I've caught was around eighteen-inches long.

Spotted gar

First, we prep the gar fishing area by leaving a spotlight on the water off the pier for a few nights to bring out the gar. Gar are surface feeders—the light brings the bugs and the bugs bring the gar.

Treble hooks

On gar fishing nights, I take a good nap in the afternoon. Then around 10 or 11 p.m., I dress all in black, with a black hoodie, so the gar won't see me standing in the shadows on the pier. They are very skitzy—if they see you, they will bolt.

I defrost some bait shrimp and grab my gar fishing rig. It's a dark colored fishing pole with a treble hook on the end and no weights.

I spray myself head-to-toe with insect repellant because the mosquitoes will be ferocious, and every bite becomes a welt on me! Then, I tiptoe out to the pier.

I thread a shrimp on the hook, let out some line, and splash the shrimp around on the surface of the water. Nothing! The river symphony is in full swing—frog chorus accompanied by chirping crickets, and of course, the constant annoying buzz of thousands of mosquitos all trying to get to me. But I don't care about the bugs. I even eat a few accidentally. I'm busy watching for the gar. I keep splashing the shrimp on the water surface, changing the pace. Nothing!

Then, a shadow catches my eye off to the right. Slowly, slowly, the gar start to appear. Several of them, lurking near the edge of the brush, in the shadows. You can see them! It's amazing to actually be able to watch the fish and see how they are interacting with your bait. Usually when you go fishing, you have to guess at what is going on under there and what the fish are doing. Here you can see them just below the surface and adjust what you are doing to their reactions. Gar fishing at night is truly a magical experience—an interactive communication with another species.

I splash the shrimp a little more frantically, then pause, then splash a little again. One of the gar is curious. He starts swimming out towards the shrimp. I move the bait a little closer to his long nose. *Splish splash,* goes the shrimp. Then I move the shrimp away from him along the water, as though it's swimming away. He cannot resist! Like a miniature of the great white shark in Jaws, he is pure instinct now. You can almost see him trembling as his raw predatory urge takes over. He MUST get that shrimp. He accelerates. He lunges. He bites! The shrimp is gone.

But here's the trick for gar. They have very boney mouths, so you can't just jerk the hook to set it, as you would for many softer mouthed fish. You have to let them taste the bait for a while. If you jerk too soon, they will just spit it out. So he starts to swim away with my shrimp and I let out a bit more line, so he doesn't get suspicious. He swims several feet, and then, when I guess that he has finally swallowed the shrimp, I jerk the line to set the hook.

I've got him! He goes wild, flailing and making a huge ruckus! It's hard to hold on to my rod, he's such a maniac! Flipping his long body this way and that, the water splashing around him as I do my best to reel him in. What a fighter! And then, suddenly, he's gone. He's flipped himself off. Got away … Darn!

I kind of doubt that any other gar will be around after all that commotion, but I wait a few minutes and decide to try one more time. I bait my hook and dangle the shrimp in the water under the light. No moving shadows. No torpedo-like gar shapes. Then, out of the left corner of my eye, I see something floating towards the pier. It looks like a log. In the shadows beyond the light's circle, it's hard to see any detail.

As the log gets closer, I see that it's actually a small alligator, coming to see what all the fuss was about! Silently and slowly, he comes near. I'm safe up on the pier, but realize that any gar in his right mind will have left the vicinity by now. So much for gar fishing! Figured I'd go to bed. But then I thought, *I wonder if the gator likes shrimp…*

So, I kept working the shrimp on the water. The gator floated in closer and closer. Finally, he was near enough. I tossed the shrimp towards his nose. *WHAM!* The gator bit the shrimp in about one second flat! I jerked the line and he was caught! Luckily, he was just a little guy—about three-feet long, or he would have broken my line. But three feet of solid muscle was now thrashing around on the end of my fishing pole! I frantically pulled out my cell phone, while struggling to hold on to the rod. Good thing Larry was on speed dial! When he answered, I just yelled, "Help!!"

Larry came running out of the house and onto the pier, barefoot, as usual. He grabbed our long dip net and as soon as I was able to wrestle the gator close enough, he swooped down and dipped it up in the net. He grabbed the little guy behind the head, removed the hook, and threw it back in the river.

I asked him, "Aren't we going to eat him?" After all, this is a guy who walks through the zoo pointing to all kinds of critters, saying, "THAT'S good eatin'!" And gator is good meat.

Larry replied, "I don't like to kill babies. We'll let him grow up a little and eat him next year."

The Flats (1983)

One more story about gators, then I'll move on to something else. There are so many alligators around here these days, that there really are a lot of gator stories to tell. First of all, let me explain what the "flats" are. In this case, it is two large areas of swamp, upper and lower flats, several miles up the Guadalupe River from my home. Some areas of the delta stay wet most of the time. The flats are two such areas. Streams snake through the area, and this helps keep the flats marshy the year around. The flats cover several square miles each.

During February through April, when there is significant rain, the flats are especially full of water and fish too! The bulk of these fish is buffalo, the predominant fish in the river. The buffalo is basically considered a trash fish because they are boney, but they are good eating. They range up to twenty-five pounds, but what I typically caught, averaged ten to twelve.

Each year, as a commercial fisherman, I caught about 50,000 pounds of buffalo, plus a few gar, that were also profitable. A lot of fish for one freelancer, huh? Buffalo didn't bring a premium price, but I made money due to volume. I caught, cleaned, and iced them in an insulated box 12x6x4 feet that I had on a trailer.

When the box was full, I hauled them to various cities including Laredo, Dallas, Shreveport, Baton Rouge, and Austin. Some of these trips were quite long at four-hundred miles, one direction. I made many 800-mile roundtrips in a single day. These were long days, but luckily it was only once a week.

I could make $500-1,000 a week, which was good money back then, but the work was back-breaking and time-consuming. I was making money though, so I did what I needed to do.

Let's say it's a typical day around the first of March. The weather is intermittently warming, it's raining on a regular basis, and the river is up a bit. There is water in the flats, and it is teeming with buffalo getting ready for spawning, which generally occurs in April. It's daylight, and I'm in my boat maneuvering into the flats through a narrow and brushy stream. My gill nets are out and I'm filling my boat with fish. Typically, I would catch around 800 pounds.

When the fish were running well, I filled my boat with buffalo on a single morning run. Keep in mind that I'm in a sixteen-foot-long boat that is four feet

Buffalo

across on the bottom. The sides spread out to about five and a half feet wide. The boat level full would be 2,000 pounds of fish, and I've had it this full more than once. This is quite a load and is a slow run back home, but at least the trip is downstream. The trip is a half hour to the nets, but nearly an hour to get back home because the boat bogs down in the water due to the weight of the fish.

When April rolls around, there will be rain and the river will be on the rise more often than not. Buffalo crowd into the flats, all vying for space to lay their eggs in the reeds of the cane. They get so thick that you can literally catch them with your hands. Square miles of nothing but water and fish, the water turning a maroon color due to the breeding process. Yellow eggs and white sperm pouring into the water from the fish. Don't ask me why it appeared maroon—I don't know, but that's what it looked like to me.

I'd lean over the side of the boat in some of the channels and lay my hands in the water feeling for the fish. They would swim right into my waiting hands where I'd grab them and sling them into the boat. Imagine catching ten- and fifteen-pound fish with your hands. Quite fun!

This particular morning, however, I was running a little light. An alligator got to one of my nets first. However, he didn't get caught. He was too big for the webbing to hold him, but the netting was too strong for him to get the fish out of the net so he could eat them. What the gator did was bite each fish numerous times trying to get it out of the net, and when he was unsuccessful, he moved to the next fish and repeated the process until every fish in the net was dead.

I removed the dead fish from the net and tossed them downstream. I hoped the big gator would follow the dead fish and leave my net alone. After three days, he finally did leave.

After getting the fish out of all my nets, I headed home. The sun was getting high, and the path out of the flats was narrow. There were moccasins in the limbs taking in the early morning sun as I drove through the gauntlet. Some of the snakes were as big around as my arm and were passing within striking range of me. I leaned away from them as I squeezed through the brush. It was scary, and though they were not likely to strike out at me, the possibility did exist. They never did over the many years this happened, but the chills they give me thinking they could, continues to pop up in my mind on occasion.

The day was not over by a long shot when I got home. In fact, the work was just beginning. The fish had to be gutted, washed, weighed, and iced down. Then the mess needed to be cleaned up, not just where the fish were cleaned, but the boat from end to end. Fish slime, blood, and guts make a big mess, but fish scales, sticks, and leaves always plug up drain holes in the boat to complicate the process. That doesn't even take into account the weather.

There was one time I recall when I sat cleaning fish for an hour, while it rained two and a half inches during the same period of time, and lightning was streaking overhead. There I sat in my slicker suit, dry as could be on the inside, but water streaming down my face as I worked. The work didn't stop just due to a little rain, even if the rain was a couple of inches an hour.

One day I was in the flats fishing when I heard what sounded like a herd of cattle running through brush. When I looked up, there was a swirling cloud of debris from a twister headed straight for me. I had no place to go, so I sat, waited, and watched. It was not much more than a dust devil, but it was quite a large one, big enough that it could flip my boat, I imagined. I didn't think getting out of the boat was such a good idea. I felt my best option would be to lay in the bottom of the boat. Luckily, the twister missed me by a good hundred feet. I sighed, cranked up the motor, and got the hell out of there with my load of fish.

On another trip into the flats, I had finished my morning run and was headed home with about 800 pounds of fish. After I'd made it through the narrowest part of my exit route where all the snakes hung out, I came around a corner, and there sat a boat with two game wardens in it. I don't know what they were doing just sitting there, but they were on the outside of my turn, I was going about half-throttle, and I was going downstream. This meant I was going to hit them no matter what I did.

You should have seen their faces when I slammed into the side of them. Their faces turned a clammy white, their eyes were big as golf balls, and their mouths hung wide open, both knowing they were in the wrong place at the wrong time.

The side of my boat slammed into the side of theirs. I made the turn I needed to make, jumped my boat and motor over a log across the waterway, and continued on my way. I never saw them again and never heard anything from anyone about the incident. I laugh every time I think of this, especially after what their comrades did to me a few years later due to new regulations. The Texas Parks and Wildlife Department is constantly changing regulations to limit what commercial fishermen can and cannot do, but that is another story for another time—or quite possibly for me, another rant!

Not Enough Water (1975)

Now, let's go downstream from where I live and out into the shallow waters of Guadalupe Lake (aka Mission Lake). It is about four miles from my home to what we call New Cut, which runs out into the lake. It is called New Cut because the channel to the open waters of the lake was made a relatively short time ago, maybe a hundred to two-hundred years or so back. It is also known as Traylor Cut. It seems like many areas around here have multiple names. What a place is called depends upon who you ask.

Guadalupe Lake is brackish water, but it never gets very salty most of the year. Only during a drought does salt water creep this far back into the estuary.

At normal tide and normal rainfall, the lake is, at best, four to five feet deep in the middle. The majority of the area is below the three-foot range. It may be shallow, but it is very good for fishing. The lake is about three-square miles and adjoins Guadalupe Bay. Only an imaginary line separates the two.

The bayous of the Guadalupe River delta are Goff, Hog, and Schwings. All three drain into Guadalupe Lake. Another significant ditch is Mamie's slough, which also dumps into Guadalupe Lake. It runs up to Alligator Slide Lake where it dead ends. Large catfish like to feed in shallow water at night, and this shallow lake can be a very good fishing spot when the water is right.

After wrapping up the end of our Fall shrimping season, usually around the end of October, we begin fishing for catfish. The fish are out in the brackish water this time of year, so we start fishing for catfish in Guadalupe Lake. This time of year, however, cold fronts chill the shallow waters of the lake, which drives the fish toward the warmer waters of the river and bayous.

We then follow the fish upstream to wherever they decide to migrate. The fish make their way into the lower Guadalupe River, and by early spring, the spawning fish make their way well up the Guadalupe and San Antonio Rivers.

Around the mouths of New Cut and Schwings bayou, there are several small ditches with no names. Over the years, flooding has changed the route of these ditches many times, and therefore the path we take our boats to and from Guadalupe Lake has changed as well. Many spots are very shallow, littered with logs, stumps, and abandoned crab pots, making travel into and out of the lake difficult. This is especially true when a fresh norther has blown in and the lake is very shallow because the north wind takes the tide out.

One such a day, after an early morning of fishing, I was headed back to the river. I hit a submerged log and lost my boat speed. I didn't have enough water to get my boat back on plane, where the boat scoots on the surface of the water like water skiing. It takes only about ten inches of water to stay on top, but twice that much to get it back to plane. I was stuck.

I started paddling, but changed my route. I took a shortcut, which would get me back to the deeper water in a much shorter distance, but I risked the water getting too shallow. I couldn't tell how shallow the water was from where I was at. I eventually got to the point of no return, and the boat was on the mud in three inches of water. It was only a hundred yards to deeper water, but I had only one choice to get there—get out and push the boat.

I was going to get wet and muddy, but that was still the best option. So, I did what I had to do; I got out in the mud and pushed. I maneuvered the boat around the logs I could see sticking out of the water and felt many more with my feet that were not sticking up. It was a good thing for the completely submerged logs, because without them it would have been much more difficult to push the boat because there seemed to be no bottom to the mud. Though there were only three or four inches of water, I sank so far in the mud that my head was just barely above the surface. If I'd have turned loose of the boat, the mud might have sucked me up, and I would never have been heard from again.

A half-hour after getting out of the boat, I was in water deep enough I could get back in. I was a mess, and I was certainly tired, but I was headed back home at a good clip. Just another day in the swamp.

Was the trip worth it? Of course, it was. I had my fifty pounds of catfish, I was no worse for wear, and I was not hurt in the least. This kind of thing builds muscle and character. It also makes you think about what happened, and you remember where that log was that you hit, which caused the problem in the first place.

Another day when I was fishing in the shallow waters of Guadalupe Lake, the wind was quite stiff, but the tackle needed to be run, and the fish taken off, so they wouldn't die on the trotlines.

The trotlines we fished with consisted of a main line with monofilament leaders and a hook at the end of each. The leaders were spaced about six feet apart. We cut long poles along the riverbank, hauled them to the lake, stuck them in the mud bottom, and tied on the main line. A normal trotline had about thirty-five hooks.

These trotlines are no longer legal. The Texas Parks & Wildlife Department tell us how to set out our trotlines, what kind of hooks to use, and what bait we can use. They even tell us we can't fish out there on weekends. I could really get on a rant here, but that is for another day, another time.

As I was making my way along the main line taking off fish and re-baiting the hooks, the main line slipped out of my hand and the hook caught in my finger. The wind blew me, and the boat, away from the trotline but the hook held on. I was holding the weight of the boat and myself in thirty mile-per-hour wind by the hook in the finger of my outstretched arm. I grabbed at the monofilament and managed to pull the leader to grab hold of the main line again. Then I was able to remove the very painful hook deeply embedded in my fortunately cold and partially numb finger. It was still extremely painful. I ripped the hook out, squeezed as much blood out of the wound as I could to clean the puncture, and went on with my fishing.

My hand was sore, but that was the punishment for my negligence. That was the only time I recall having lost control of the main line. The wound was sore for several days as a constant reminder to take more care when the wind is up.

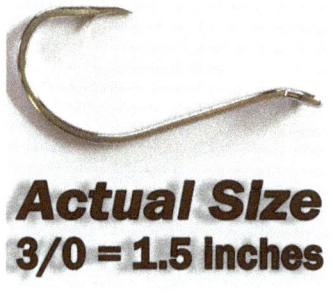

The hook size I use is 3/0 (pronounced three aught). They are relatively small compared to what is used in salt water. The parts to a hook are the point, barb, shank, and eye. I think you can guess which are which.

It doesn't take a large hook to catch and hold catfish. I have caught and landed fish up to fifty pounds with this size hook. Notice the barb near the point. This helps keep fish on the hook. Otherwise, the fish can shake the hook out of their mouth and you will lose many of the fish you catch. This barb was also why the hook in my finger was so painful.

Negligence, lack of knowledge, and sometimes just the dumb luck of being in the wrong place at the wrong time are great teachers. When you live in a swamp, you have to pay attention constantly. As I have said many times: "What you learn today, will determine how well you live tomorrow." This includes more than financial rewards. It includes avoiding repeating painful injuries as well.

Homer's Goat (1965)

As I told you earlier, my mom and dad divorced when I was twelve, and me and my two sisters moved to nearby Port Lavaca. My mother was a great businesswoman who, with no help from anyone else for several years, got into the bar business. She made good money with her first business after Hurricane Carla in 1961. This led her to buy two more bars, and she did well.

My mother loved fishing, and she was totally the reason I became a swamp person. She re-married in 1964 when I was sixteen. My mother, step-dad, my sisters, and I moved to the banks of the Guadalupe River. I became a resident of the Guadalupe delta swamp rather than just a frequent visitor. So, let me tell you a little more about this unique lady. I am one of a kind, as she was, and that's pretty damned unique.

She took an interest in shrimping. She bought a small boat and painted it pink. She and her all-female crew made up of family and friends, ran the boat. And they ran the boat very well, so she bought another and another. I think she had five at one point, but eventually semi-retired with one. She liked fishing for catfish more and concentrated on running the one shrimp boat with her new husband during the summer and fall, then moved on to catching catfish during the winter and spring. She earned the title "Catfish Mama".

When we moved to the Guadalupe River, we had two neighbors. My grandpa (Mom's dad) lived on the other side of the highway two-hundred yards away. An unrelated couple lived a hundred and fifty yards in the other direction. The couple's son, his wife, and their kids lived alongside in a trailer house. I will call the son Homer.

At the time, I think Homer was in his thirties. He drank a lot and was nice on occasion, but was mostly obnoxious, especially when he drank.

Well, Homer had a goat, chickens, geese and ducks, and guinea hens. The guineas were noisy, his geese and ducks pooped all over our porch on a regular basis, and the goat ate Mama's garden.

Mom warned Homer about the geese and ducks many times, but they always seemed to return to our porch. They made a mess, but they caused no real harm. The goat, on the other hand, ate Mama's garden and this was a real problem with devastating damage. The goat also seemed to like standing on top of our picnic table and pooping there.

My mother and my step-dad grew an extensive garden with potatoes, carrots, onions, squash, beans, cucumbers, and plenty of cabbage, lettuce, and greens. Now you can imagine how much damage a goat can cause to a garden. Even if you can't imagine, I assure you, it *was* devastating.

My mother warned Homer to keep his goat home on numerous occasions, but repeatedly the goat returned. Finally, my mother threatened Homer that she'd kill the goat if he did not keep it home and out of her garden. Again, and again though, the animal returned and always headed straight for the garden. Homer kept telling my mother he didn't believe she would kill his goat, but one day, she awoke in a bad mood and Homer's goat was in her garden. She grabbed her gun and shot it.

That was the day Mama got Homer's goat, and we had a barbecue that weekend. Yep, that's what she did, all right! It was eating her garden and making messes. Well, he couldn't say she didn't warn him. Mama even invited Homer to the barbecue, but for some reason, he didn't attend.

At the request of a friend, I am including more short stories about my mother. The first is her love of gambling in Las Vegas.

She played the slots at the Sands Hotel & Casino until they tore it down. She stopped going to Vegas, but she loved to play.

She never worried about losing, but she had won so much during a lucky streak that ran for several years. She won around a quarter of a million dollars, mostly in two slot tournaments including the Rich & Famous Slot Tournament. She became a celebrity in Vegas. I have heard more stories about her winnings than I can count. She was one lucky lady.

Mama bought a smaller version of a slot machine to put on the entry porch to her home. This slot machine got a lot of attention from all who visited, and if Mama got an itch to play the slots and she didn't have a trip planned, she didn't have far to go to scratch the itch. She never quit going to real casinos though.

She wasn't going to win anything on her own slot machine. She loved taking casino money, and she did exactly that for many years.

When the Sands was torn down, she started playing in Coushatta, Louisiana. Her luck continued there, and they never got back all the money she won at their one-arm bandits.

Mama loved to have fun, and she especially loved her grandkids, who gave her the most pleasure. They had fun with some talking toys she bought on a regular basis. One was a talking deer head, but the most fun was with a talking fish on a plaque, singing, "Gimme back that filet of fish . . ." The kids enjoyed it, but the grandkids went nuts over the talking fish. One of the kids would push the button, and the blue plastic fish bent in the middle to turn and face outward as it began to sing. The mouth moved, and the kids would laugh and giggle until it finished its song. Someone always reached for the button repeatedly. As many times as it was played, I don't see how the toy lasted so many years.

Talking plastic fish

The talking deer head was a head-mount you would expect to see in a deer hunter's home on the wall. It was a very good replica too. It wouldn't fool any

Talking deer head

grown-up, but it did fool the younger kids. It scared some until they got used to it. Mom mostly used it to play hoaxes on adults. It came with a portable microphone for her to talk for the deer and it also sang pre-recorded songs like 'Rawhide'. Its mouth moved, its ears wiggled, and the head turned and bowed to the voices or music. I even got a kick out of it myself.

Mama had a lot of fun with grown-ups too, especially with strangers. The deer head played a big part in her fun. And she wasn't bashful at all. She would invite new people into her home and announce herself, "Hi, I'm Virginia; Virgin for short, but not for long."

Other talking and singing toys included a singing Christmas tree and a Santa Claus in his red car. Mama loved entertaining the kids. Maybe that was the reason everyone in the family grew up happy. There was always something to laugh at, and often Mom was the source of the laughs.

I know you're going to like this story.

My mother and step-dad always had a lot of meat to grind. They were always butchering something—deer, goats, or hogs—to make sausage, burger patties, or whatever. It seemed like when they butchered, much of the meat was ground up.

So, when you have a lot of meat to grind up, how do you grind it as fast as you can and with the least amount of effort? You hook the meat grinder up to the tractor, of course. You didn't know that?

Many people thought it was strange to use a tractor to grind meat, but believe me, it worked very well and quickly. Sometimes they were processing fifty to a hundred pounds of meat, but no matter how much they had, it didn't take long.

My step-dad made an attachment that hooked up fast and easy. He'd crank up the tractor, hook up the grinder, and get the meat going. Before they knew it, all the meat was processed and in the house. The cleanup of the grinder was easy, and they didn't even get tired or work up a sweat. The meat was still cold and ready to be processed into whatever they wanted.

My mother and step-dad made a lot of sausage patties, sausage links, summer sausage, bologna, and hamburger. They smoked some of it in a commercial grade smoker they purchased, but no matter what they did with the meat, thanks to the tractor and Leonard's ingenuity, the grinding part didn't take long.

Mama loved to make things out of wood she found around and in the river. These included clocks, and the heaviest coffee table I've ever seen. Leonard assisted with cutting the wood to her exact specifications. Then she sanded, varnished, and finished her crafts.

Homemade clock from slice of cypress tree

Homemade clock from slice of cypress tree

A very heavy coffee table

Gambling is in My Blood (2016)

Mama isn't the only one who likes to gamble. I guess it runs in the blood, and a little of her luck has also rubbed off on me, but I am an introvert—I don't like crowds. That said, I love Las Vegas, and that has been my 'home away from home' for ten years now. I used to go to Vegas more often, but these days once or twice a year seems to be enough. I love playing in the World Series of Poker there, and all the sights and sounds which go with the game and the city.

It's a three-hour drive to San Antonio, where I usually fly out. When I hit SA, I am thrust into heavy traffic, a crowded airport, then a full plane of travelers. I wait in lines and then sit for a couple of hours in a cramped seat. More lines in Las Vegas, but I finally make it to the Rio Hotel & Casino where the WSOP is held every year, and I make it up to my suite. Finally, a little space. I do not stay there long though. Shortly, I'm off to the tables.

I usually hit the single-table satellites to see if I can win my way into the bigger tournaments. I did poorly last year. The games

One-and-a-half-million in poker chips

were up and down, and I made no tournament buy-ins. I had to pay out of my pocket for all the games I played. I couldn't win a buy-in to save my life. I played in three World Series bracelet events and several deep-stack tournaments. My dream has always been to win a WSOP bracelet. This status symbol has always been my top prize, though the money would be nice as well, generally in the quarter-million to half-a-million-dollar range.

What could possibly get an introvert into the crowded poker rooms? Texas No-limit Hold'em is a great game. I have been playing poker most of my life and simply love the game for the thrill of winning, which I have achieved numerous times, just not last year. I love playing poker with professional or good poker players. Last year, as has happened many times in the past, I ran into multiple novice players. These guys will kill you when they get lucky after making a foolish, low-percentage play. In the long term, reckless play will never be profitable, but in the short term, I have witnessed some extremely lucky and profitable behavior. I consider myself a good player and try to play well at all times, but luck is a big part of poker, and without it, you cannot win. Lady luck didn't seem to follow me around last year, and I went home a *loser*. But, there is always next year!

I always have fun though, win or lose. The food is great, and the eye candy is always pleasant. The floor servers wear skimpy costumes, and there are usually dancers who perform regularly. These gals don't wear much. There are pools, spas, shows, and so many other attractions in Las Vegas. Everyone should go there at least once, introvert or extrovert.

A side note, as much as I loved the trip and the experience, home sure felt good when I arrived back in my swamp. I think Mama always felt the same. She always remained a swamp dweller just like I have become. It's not the money that makes life great, it's where you live and how you live. I've enjoyed Las Vegas for many years, but home is always where the heart is, even if it is a swamp, but for me, especially because it *is* a swamp.

Mama Told Me ... (2012)

My best friend asked me to write this story because it made him laugh. It is a story about something I learned from my mama many years ago: 'Don't take crap from other people'. Living alone with my mom when I was young, I learned a little more from her than I probably would have otherwise.

I post this true story in tribute to my mother for Mother's Day. She will be 93 years old in a couple of weeks. She never took crap from anyone and everyone else knew it, or if they didn't, they soon learned if they gave her a problem.

If you take crap from other people, people are always going to dish it out your direction. Are you willing to take it for the rest of your life? I wasn't. When I get it, I can deal with it too. Maybe that is one of the problems with many people these days. There is a lot of crap in the world, mostly government and large corporations. Do you take it, or do you fight back?

Living in the country has a major drawback in our modern electronic age. The Internet is a challenge at best. Remember dial-up? Thank goodness that is no longer around. I thought satellite was the answer to my problems, and it was fairly fast, but around here it has been unreliable and expensive. Maybe the problem was with the provider. Anyway, it didn't work very well.

Speed has always been the primary concern. I've tried many things to boost speed while keeping the cost at bay. I thought Sprint had the answer. What I got from them was a nightmare.

Sprint had a plug-in device which they claimed would give me reliable, fast internet service anywhere through the local cell phone service tower. I had a Sprint phone and the phone worked well. I originally went with Sprint because the cell tower was near my home.

Well, I bought the Sprint plug-in device, disconnected the satellite service, and plugged the device in, and voila, internet service. Was it fast? No! Not much better than dial-up. Was it dependable? No! It kept going out and stayed off for hours. It did not stay connected for more than a couple of hours, then I was out of service. The little module felt hot to the touch. This I suspected was the reason the device stopped working.

It did this over and over, and no way was weather a factor. It was just a bad device. Sprint replaced the unit, and it was no better, though they checked it at the store and said it was working fine. That darned thing just wouldn't work in my area even though I could easily see the Sprint cell tower on the hill from my front door.

I contacted the Sprint home office, cancelled the service, and tried to get them to refund my money. Well, they would not, and on top of that, I was slapped with a $200 early disconnect fee. Bullshit!

I immediately contacted a new satellite service provider and got new service. Satellite internet is the only option, and the new service is not what it claims, but the best I've had.

Back to Sprint, I threatened to sue them if they did not refund my money for the device, rescind the early disconnect fee, and reimburse me for phone charges for the device. I did not ask for much, only what I figured the device had cost me—all in all, less than $500.

How did they respond? They ignored me, completely and repeatedly! I did a little research and filed a lawsuit in District Court, as the Sprint Home Office is located in another state. I did this without a lawyer, but was ready to hire one if necessary. Filing a lawsuit is easy with just a little knowledge I picked up on the internet.

As soon as the Sheriff's Office delivered the summons to Sprint, I got a phone call from Sprint's lawyers. They wanted to settle out of court, and immediately. We cut a deal over the phone, and the lady said it would take a couple of weeks for me to get the check. It took two days! I dropped the lawsuit.

Case two in point: A few weeks ago, I ordered some netting to cover my garden and some plastic zip ties to attach the netting to the fencing. The netting was perfect, but when I tried to attach it to the fencing with the zip ties, many of the ties broke in my hands, and many more broke while attaching. They were extremely brittle like they were very old from sitting in a hot warehouse somewhere for years, if not decades.

I had purchased the ties through Amazon and wrote to the supplier through Amazon about their product. The ties only cost $11, and the supplier offered to pay $4 for the bad ties. I didn't want money; I wanted good ties. They offered $5 and then $6 as a refund, but I insisted I didn't want money. They also said I had to remove the bad feedback from Amazon before they would send the money. I told them that wasn't going to happen and that the feedback would only get worse if I didn't get my new zip ties. As much hassle as they were giving me it wasn't about the money anymore. I wanted new and useable ties to attach my netting. Then, they asked if I wanted them to send me new ties. Duh! I got the new ties a few days later, and they are not brittle and look to be a size larger. Perfect!

Why in hell would they do what they did? Are they stupid? Why did they think they could send me crap and then pay me off for anything less than the full cost of the ties? Why would they even try? Did they think I was stupid? I guess there really are a lot of stupid people out there. This reminds me of something you should learn right now as I have. If you don't protect yourself, who will? Don't be afraid to scream, holler, and stomp your feet if someone tries to screw you.

It is a little extra work to deal with companies who want to jerk you around, but the satisfaction of beating them when they only want to screw you is worth it. So, the next time you don't get what you pay for, don't take the crap. If you do, the crap will grow exponentially for everyone. Maybe my actions will save someone else from a big business headache down the road.

Mama's Recipes (2017)

When I get on stories about Mama, you know how it is, there's always another to tell. Or maybe you don't. There are more stories about my mother than most mothers I suspect. I almost wrote a book about mine a few years back. Maybe one day I will, as there are really a lot of unique stories to tell. I can't do it here though.

This story is going to be a better one than the last. It is about her cooking, and I'm going to give you some recipes. Some of these recipes are as old as I am, but there are some newer ones, too, that are just as good. A case in point is her quick cobbler. Maybe it can be made a little better the old-fashioned way, but not quicker, of course!

Mama had a sweet-tooth, but she knew how to satisfy the need for sugar. She made fudge for as long as I can remember. This was way back when the chocolate came in small unsweet blocks of cocoa.

Mama was always making cakes, pies, and other pastries. I say always, but it was mostly around the holidays or someone's birthday. Around our place, that was quite often.

She found the recipe for a quick cobbler somewhere. I don't know where, but at one point she began churning them out on a regular basis. The quality of the cobbler is highly dependent upon the quality of the fruit. Fresh or fresh frozen peaches work best, though the original recipe indicated canned peaches. To us country folk though, canned peaches don't even seem like real peaches; almost like a different fruit, both in texture and taste. Around here, good cooks are much like engineers—we love to change things. There are two goals: quicker or better. Rule number one though, is don't choose quicker if it significantly lowers the taste factor.

Quick Cobbler

Ingredients:

    1 stick margarine (we prefer Fleischman's® original)
    1 c. flour
    1-1/4 c. sugar
    1 c. milk

12 oz. fresh or fresh frozen peaches
2 tsp. cinnamon
3 tsp. baking powder

In a 10-inch square baking dish, melt margarine. In a sauce pan, heat peaches on low heat with ¼ c. sugar and 1 tsp. cinnamon. This will thicken them. In a mixing bowl, mix flour, remaining sugar, baking powder, and remaining cinnamon, then stir in milk. Whisk sparingly until most lumps are gone. Pour this mixture into the baking dish with the melted butter, then add hot peaches in the center. Do not stir anything. Bake at 425° for 20–25 minutes.

It's great served hot alongside a little Blue Bell® Homemade Vanilla ice cream, or your favorite vanilla.

A breakfast staple for many years was fresh homemade biscuits. We had a milk cow growing up, so there was always milk around. It was not pasteurized and didn't keep long, even in the refrigerator. Mama took the butter and curds out of the milk, and I remember my parents making all kinds of products out of the milk itself.

My dad made what was referred to as 'stink cheese', and it's appropriately named. My mother made him keep it in the garage while it was fermenting, or whatever it was doing, and he was only allowed to bring a small amount into the house when he ate it.

There was always buttermilk and whole milk around the house at various stages of deterioration. I didn't care for buttermilk at all, but it did make excellent biscuits. Milk is okay to make the biscuits too, especially if it is starting to sour a bit. Today I use buttermilk, but if I don't have any, I'll also use regular milk (or 2%, which I drink most of the time) with a tablespoon of vinegar added. The biscuits are great to sop up a little gravy, but if you put a little margarine inside, they're fine like that too.

Homemade Biscuits

Ingredients:

2 c. all-purpose flour, plus extra for preparing dough into biscuits
¼ c. vegetable oil
2 tsp. baking powder

1 tsp. salt
¼ tsp. soda
Buttermilk (or milk with 1 tbsp. 9% vinegar)

In a square metal baking pan, add vegetable oil. In a mixing bowl, mix dry ingredients and add buttermilk, or milk, until the dry ingredients just barely hold together into a thick dough. Sprinkle a little flour onto cabinet top or plastic sheet. Dig the dough out of the bowl and place it onto this layer of flour. Sprinkle a small amount of flour onto both the dough and your hand, then pat the dough flat until it's about an inch thick. Cut into biscuits using the open end of a drinking glass with a little flour on rim. Take biscuits and dip one side into the oil in the baking pan and place the other side down into the oil. This way they have oil on the top and bottom sides. When all biscuits are in the pan, bake in oven pre-heated to 450° for about fifteen minutes or until light to medium brown.

Because these biscuits don't have shortening in them, they do not get hard and will still be nearly as good as fresh for the next couple of days, if it takes that long to eat them up. Store in the refrigerator in a Ziploc plastic bag. When you need a hot biscuit, pop one in the microwave oven for twelve to fifteen seconds.

I remember eating a jar of pickled beets and getting sick on them when I was around nine years old. I don't know how I got the quart jar open at that age, but I did, and I ate almost the entire jar. The next day, I thought I was dying when I pooped what looked like blood. So, remember this if you eat too many.

From my experience, most people either love pickled beets, or they can't stand them. I don't like the taste of beets, but I do love the sweetness and tartness of them when pickled. The same is true with me for cucumbers. I don't care for raw cucumbers, but I love dill pickles—what are called hamburger dills—but also the brine pickles that Mom and Dad made most years growing up.

I don't think anyone ever named the pickled beets, but when I wrote my first novel, *Into Autumn*, Lars Lindgren made pickled beets for his neighbor and best friend's wife, Emily. Lars got Emily addicted to his beets, and she couldn't seem to go long without them. Her husband, and Lars's best friend, Reggie, would give Lars anything for the beets Emily loved so much.

So, in honor of Lars Lindgren in *Into Autumn*, I have named the pickled beets Lars's Pickled Beets, even though they were handed down from my mother and probably her mother before her. If you were to ask me how many jars of this necessity I have in the pantry right now, I'd tell you nine quarts.

The recipe and process are a little difficult, but I assure you it's not all that hard, and the finished product is well worth the effort. If you're making this recipe for the first time, however, I would plan things out before you start. Taking the lesson of the 6Ps from *Into Spring*, book two of my *Four Seasons Series*, proper preparation prevents piss poor performance.

Lars's Pickled Beets

Ingredients:

Enough beets with the tops cut off (leaving a little stub) to fill your largest pot, plus:

9% white vinegar
Sugar
Water
Whole cloves (not a secret ingredient anymore)

I can't tell you exactly how much you'll need because that depends upon how many beets you have. The recipe for the juice mixture is as follows:

1 c. water
1 c. vinegar
1 c. sugar

Simple enough, right? Sometimes I like to add a little extra sugar and vinegar—maybe an extra quarter-cup of each. The hard part is guessing how much juice you'll need for the beets you have. Also, how many quart jars the beets will fit into. As many times as I've done the recipe, I still never get it exactly right, but I always have juice left. I'm guessing, but I think a 1-1-1 recipe above will do about 1-1/2 quarts. It seems like I usually mix up about six or seven of the 1-1-1 recipes at a time and get maybe ten quarts.

You should begin by sterilizing your jars. This can be done in the dishwasher.

Beets ready to cook; Ready to can

All right, let's get started cooking the beets. The first thing you want to do is boil the beets in water in a large pot. Cook until just barely soft, as they will be cooked a bit more later. Check with a toothpick.

Dump beets in the sink to clean. The skins should just slide off. Also remove ends and any bad spots, then cut into one-inch chunks, more or less. Add beets to 1-1-1 juice mixture in a large pot and bring to a full boil.

Sterilize the lids in a shallow pot of boiling water. Place a half-dozen whole cloves into each jar. As soon as the beets get to a full boil, scoop the beets into the first jar, quickly shaking them down as you go, dip up juice quickly and fill to within a quarter-inch of the rim, give the rim a quick wipe with a damp cloth, add the lid, and tighten the band quickly. Repeat as fast as you can until all jars are filled. Most recipes include putting the jars into a hot water bath for at least ten minutes at this point. We don't. Skip this step at your own risk.

This next recipe is not actually from my mother, but she sure cooked it often. The recipe came from an ex-brother-in-law. The recipe is very simple, and if you love bacon and/or shrimp, you'll love it. It's been called goulash for as long as I can remember, though it is technically not a goulash. You call it what you like, but to me it is:

Shrimp Goulash

Ingredients:

    2 lbs. shrimp, deveined and boiled
    6-8 cups rice
    2 lg. yellow onions

1 lb. mild bacon
1 stick margarine (Fleischman's® original)
Salt
Pepper
Garlic powder or clove garlic (chopped)

I like to use a little less rice because I like more shrimp and bacon in my goulash, but sometimes I use more rice to make the dish go further. I like to use Success® rice (white) because it cooks quickly and perfectly every time. I like white rice while Ellen prefers brown rice. Often, we'll mix the two. Wild rice is good too.

The first thing you do is chop your onions into quarter- to half-inch pieces and get them cooking with the margarine in a large pot. Cut the bacon up into half- to three-quarter-inch pieces and add to the onions and margarine immediately. Let simmer a while until bacon is soft-cooked and the onions have browned slightly.

Add spices to your taste. I like heavy on the garlic, maybe three or four tablespoons of garlic powder, or numerous cloves of garlic if you choose that route. Remember, the rice will dilute the flavor. I'd go a little light on the salt and pepper. You can always add more later. You don't want the pepper to overwhelm the taste of the shrimp and bacon. Also, the bacon will have some salt and not a lot of extra will be needed.

While the spices are simmering add the boiled shrimp and stir into the mixture. Cut off heat, immediately add the drained rice to the pot, and stir up well to mix the juices throughout the rice. It is now ready to serve. This recipe will serve maybe eight to ten people depending upon how much rice you added. If I were twenty years younger, it would only serve four people like me. Often when I make this dish, this is my entire meal. Yes, I like it that much.

When my parents divorced, and we moved to Port Lavaca, my younger sister and I were left alone much of the time. My mother had to earn a living. We had a baby-sitter occasionally, but much of the time we were alone, especially after school and on weekends, and we got hungry. This is where I learned to cook. I didn't enjoy it back then, but I have since learned that I do like cooking, and I have several unique dishes. I will share one with you.

It is a one-pot dish that will serve a large family and guests. It takes two pots to prepare, and one had better be quite large because the entire recipe will end up in that one pot. I use the same one I use when I'm pickling beets.

Dirty Spaghetti

Ingredients:

- 2 lbs. ground chuck
- 2 lg. yellow onions
- 1 20 oz. can of cream of chicken soup
- 1 20 oz. can cream of mushroom soup
- 1 stick margarine (Fleischman's® original)
- 1 20 oz. pkg. spaghetti
- 1 lg. can pitted black olives
- 1 med. pkg. fresh white mushrooms
- 2 cans Rotel® tomatoes and green chilies (mild)
- 1 tbsp. salt
- 1 tbsp. black pepper
- 4 tbsp. garlic powder
- 2 tbsp. Worcestershire sauce
- 6 tbsp. Greek seasoning
- 1 tsp. Cayenne pepper (omit if you don't like it too hot)
- 2 tbsp. oregano
- 3 tbsp. ground Comino
- 2 tbsp. seasoned salt
- 1 tbsp. sage
- 2 tbsp. Italian seasoning
- 2 tbsp. Head Country Championship Seasoning, or similar multi-purpose seasoning
- 2 tbsp. Emeril's steak rub, or your favorite steak rub
- 1 tbsp. onion powder
- 2 tbsp. olive oil

If you don't have one or two of the spices, that's okay. You can swap for something similar or can modify with some of your favorite ingredients to change the flavor to suit yourself. I generally throw just about everything I have into the mix. The large number of spices add to the depth of the flavor, so if you leave out one or two, it's not going to make much difference in the taste.

To start out, add a little olive oil and a pinch of salt to some water in a large pot, and boil the spaghetti. I like to break the spaghetti in half, so it's not so long. When cooked, drain and set aside.

In a very large pot that will be capable of holding all the ingredients, and be the final pot for the dish, add the margarine, ground meat, and chopped onions. Cook over a medium heat until the meat is browned. Turn the heat to low and add the fresh sliced mushrooms, sliced black olives, and Rotel® tomatoes and chilies. Add the two cans of soup and, while it is heating, add all the remaining spices and mix thoroughly. Turn the heat back up to medium and bring to a boil. Remove from heat, add the spaghetti, and mix well. Serve immediately.

You should be able to tell from the ingredients that these aren't low-calorie meals. Swamp people don't worry about calories. We burn off whatever we eat on a daily basis, even in the wintertime. Maybe when we get old, and don't work quite as hard, we will have to pay a little more attention to what we're eating, but during most of our lives, we don't. It was nothing for me to burn 5,000 calories a day. The bigger problem was eating enough to keep from losing weight.

Everyone would maybe gain a few pounds around the holidays or birthday parties when we didn't work quite as hard, but we always burned it off shortly thereafter.

My mother hosted Easter parties every year for many years, and there were always more than two-dozen family members present. My mother and step-dad provided the main course and a few side-dishes, and they made plenty. Others brought side-dishes and a few desserts.

Everyone certainly enjoyed my mother and step-dad's cooking. I mention my step-dad here because he could fry up fresh catfish to perfection quickly in his large cast-iron pot. This was always done outside, and he often cooked up thirty to fifty pounds of fish. Everyone continued to nibble on his fish long after they were full. He took care of the barbecue too, but this was the limit of his cooking. Mama took care of the rest. And because Mama was Mama, she was eternally making certain my step-dad was doing it right—her right, not always his right.

I picked up the desire to cook somewhere along the way and really enjoyed baking breads and cakes. I still love cooking to this day. Maybe this is because no one else could replace my mother's cooking, but maybe also because I paid attention to what she did and how she enjoyed it. I'm glad I gathered up some of her recipes long before she died, so that they wouldn't die with her.

A big pot of dirty spaghetti or shrimp goulash can certainly take care of the kids and grandkids when they visit. Little else is needed or wanted. The kids like my cooking too. I had a good teacher.

You Are What You Eat! (2016)

The main reason I've written this short story is to list all the critters I've eaten that are out of the ordinary. What got me to thinking about it was a new friend I made the other day who studies genetics.

Most people have heard the phrase 'you are what you eat'. If you eat things that are good for you, your body should grow healthy and strong. I am certainly diverse in this respect. That is also likely one reason I'm so unique; or maybe I eat all these things because of my uniqueness. Either way works for me.

Most people in the U.S. eat only beef, pork, fish, crab, shrimp, chicken, turkey, and that's about it. I doubt some people utilize all of these meats. In addition to the above, I've had these delicacies:

deer	turtle	squirrel
rabbit	armadillo	meadowlark
robin	blackbird	dove
quail	octopus	eel
grasshoppers	ants	nutria
stingray	squid	geese & ducks
alligator	oysters	clams
mussels	shark	elk
cardinal	horse	crayfish

And though these are animal parts rather than an animal, they are good nevertheless: testicles, tongue, and bone marrow. Eyes are supposed to be good, but I won't eat them. I do have my limit.

And these are just the meats. I'm sure there are a few nuts, grains, and vegetables I've eaten that you've never even heard of, such as bull-nettle nuts.

Some of the above are not very good, and I no longer eat them. Whether you use the term 'non-game' or 'delicacies', some of the above meats are not what they're cracked up to be; for instance, meadowlark, cardinal (a state bird), blackbird, and nutria. Armadillo is good, but there are two diseases humans can get from them, including leprosy, so I don't mess with them anymore. You would never get the disease from eating the critter as long as it's cooked thoroughly, but the disease can be contracted while processing the animal and coming into contact with its blood and organs. While there are many armadillos around here, the risk of contracting the disease and its severity keeps me away from them.

You may or may not notice snake is not on the list. I just never got around to eating this particular critter. Eating rattlesnake is common around Texas, but though I've killed plenty, I've never eaten one. I have no plans to eat one either, though I would if I didn't have to clean and cook it, or if I was hungry enough.

So, how many of the critters in the above list have you eaten? Squid and oysters are my favorites on the list. I try to have these as often as possible.

Genes play a large role in who you are too, and as you grow and develop, your cells, genes included, are affected by diet. Then, as you procreate, you pass your genes to your offspring. Are they healthy, or are you passing on adversely affected cells? In what condition are the genes you got from your parents?

Offspring generally tend to follow the same path as their parents, at least in their early years. If you pass on adversely affected genes, then your kids tend to aggravate their genetics even further, creating a downward spiral in their inherent capabilities. If on the other hand, you do your very best to eat well and take care of your body, an upward spiral can be created.

You might be asking yourself about now, how does this relate to me and the swamp? The answer is simple. There are many things that can enter your body other than through your mouth. This is especially true in my swamp. I grew up in and near the Guadalupe River delta and have always been exposed to dangers. Most have resulted in chemicals, bacteria, and germs injected or absorbed into my body in one fashion or another.

My usual foot attire

I've trampled around in the marshy area, and also a creek that runs through the property. There was a lot of stagnant water around. Much of the time I was barefoot, just as I am most of the time now. All sorts of thorny trees, shrubs, vines, and other plants constantly poked me. I also got cut on a regular basis. This is still the case.

Thorns have injected me with their poisons, and the punctures and cuts provided an easy entry point for all sorts of germs prevalent around horses, cattle, and numerous wild animals. Then there were biting insects of numerous varieties, which were a constant bother. On top of these, was the poison ivy, poison oak, and sumac. Lastly, off the top of my head, I can remember getting finned by freshwater and saltwater fish, bitten by crabs, and stung by a variety of jellyfish, bees, and wasps.

When I got old enough to help my dad do chores, my body was subjected to a whole new set of chemicals. Among these were cattle spray, brush- and insect-control sprays, oils, and leaded gasoline—to name a few. These must have been absorbed into my body. What was their effect?

I worked hard, ate hearty, though maybe not quite as healthy as I should have, but probably not as bad as many people. I do eat a lot more vegetables now than I have most of my life, but it's probably a little late to be concerned with genetics. I'm not, however, in such poor shape as many people my age. I'm strong and still work harder than most in my age group.

So, what does all this mean for my health? I seldom get sick. I'm never depressed. I feel good most of the time—maybe a little arthritis here and there, and a little joint pain occasionally due to injuries I've had. Most of my life I worked and played in the sun from daylight to dark with no sunscreen and wearing only a T-shirt at most. I've gone to bed more times than I can count, feeling like a microwave cooked potato, radiating a day's stored-up energy. It was inevitable that I'd get skin cancer.

In July of 2017, I was diagnosed with a squamous cell carcinoma on my neck behind my left ear. The dermatologist cut a two-square-inch oval chunk out of my skin. An examination of the removed area showed they got it all before the doc even sewed me up. Good news!

I do know one thing; I don't worry about the few mosquito bites or fire ant stings I get on a regular basis—daily, at times. They don't bother me much or for long. Ellen, my significant other, on the other hand, gets a few ant bites and they really get nasty. They even make her a little sick if she gets more than one or two. Mosquito stings make big welts on her skin and often bother her for days. She was raised in the city, and she's not used to all the insects she now must deal with on a regular basis.

Ellen tries to get me to eat better, and she does, but I need to have at least some of what I've been used to much of my life. This includes many things with a lot of preservatives in them, which she tries to avoid. I tell her that at my age, I need all the preservatives I can get.

I think my body has been so accustomed to fighting off this and that, it's why few things bother me anymore. Killer bees twice, a copperhead in the air conditioner condenser, which bit me on the hand; and it seems like every time I turn around, I'm bleeding. Very little seems to bother me like it does Ellen.

So, what does this tell you about what you eat and are subjected to, and your genes? I'm not proof of anything, but I think that "What doesn't kill you, makes you stronger." I think you need to keep your weight at least close to normal, work hard at manual labor even if it's only in your backyard, and eat the best you can. Then, with a little luck, and some good genes, you should live a long, healthy, and hopefully happy life.

We are evolving and changing as a people. That is after all what life is ultimately about. If we don't kill each other off or destroy this planet, we will ultimately all end up as little gray men and women with shiny black eyes, flying around in our tiny little spaceships. Something to look forward to, huh?

Recently, I awoke from a dream that was still quite vivid. This might make some people sick, but what I was dreaming about was eating a mouse—alive. You might ask why in the world would I be dreaming about eating a small live rodent? The reason is not so far-fetched as you might think.

As I told you, I have eaten probably more different kinds of meat than you have to start with, but maybe more so because of a couple of television shows that I watch. The first is *Survivor*®, which I have been watching since the show first hit the tube. Then, more recently, *Naked and Afraid*®.

I went as far as filling out the application for *Survivor*® but never sent it in. I finally decided I did not have the endurance to do well. Though I loved the show, I decided to pass it up. I've wished I hadn't ever since.

The reason I eventually decided to pass up *Survivor*® was due to an on-the-job accident on December 8, 2000, in which I nearly died and should have died. I've have had residual effects from the injuries ever since. I've included that story in this book under the title *The Day My World Blew Up in My Face, Literally*. This story does not occur in or around my swamp, but I thought it should be included. I've come really close to dying four times in my life—more than anyone should, but again, that's just my opinion.

Anyway, I've eaten a lot of things that a person would not ordinarily eat, including squirrels, which in fact are rodents. I eat them cooked though. They are quite delicious, and I wouldn't hesitate to eat them right now.

Back to the mouse, I remember the thing squirming in my mouth, the bones crunching as I chewed, while it tried to scratch its way out with its tiny claws. I could

Squirrels on the pit

feel the muscles quivering as it was dying and sliding down my throat when I woke up. Am I giving you the shivers with this story? Yeah, it gives them to me too.

When I was heavily considering getting on *Naked and Afraid*®, I would eat ants, grasshoppers, and seeds off weeds. They really didn't taste bad. A lot different than I thought. Mostly, they were just a little scratchy going down. The taste didn't bother me. I don't know about you, but I'm getting a little hungry. How about a bowl of raw oysters? Maybe just a ham sandwich, this time.

Super Dogs (1975)

Not long after I got married and moved to the swamp on the Guadalupe River Delta, my ex and I acquired two dogs. We named them Willie and Wendy. They were super dogs in every respect.

My ex picked the terrier mix puppies up at a local pound one spring. We were soon heavily into our shrimping season, and we took the young puppies onto the boat with us. Willie was aggressive towards the crabs he found crawling around the boat every time I brought the net in and dumped our catch. It didn't take him long to learn they would pinch him if given a chance.

Willie wasn't about to let a mindless crustacean get the best of him. He learned what would hurt him and soon found that if he bit one of the pincers, the crab would let go of it and only have one with which to protect itself. Willie removed the second pincer easily with a quick bite, and the crab was harmless.

Crabs can turn loose of any of their legs. If a leg is damaged, the crab lets it go, then over time, grows a new one—if they stay alive, that is. Willie usually finished his task by killing the crab.

Crabs are quite quick, and the challenge was to get the first pincer removed. It sometimes took ten or fifteen minutes of careful maneuvering to finally accomplish this task. But when this was completed, Willie removed the other pincer in short order and crunched his teeth into the back of the crab to kill it. Game over!

We got the male and female puppies so they could breed and provide us with more dogs, but as it turned out, Wendy had a heart condition, and she also could not have puppies. By the time we found this out though, we no longer cared about her having little ones. We only cared that she was so loveable and playful with our children. The young kids pulled at Wendy's ears and tail, but she never growled. She took everything in stride. It was as if our kids were hers as well. Willie was a little rowdier than Wendy, but both were good with our young kids.

Wendy was never rowdy, but was highly protective of our family in her gentle way. I remember one winter after killing a deer, I hung the carcass in a tree to chill overnight before processing. Wendy laid at the base of the tree all night guarding the deer. No raccoon or opossum was going to get at our food. How did she know this?

As gentle as Willie was towards our kids, learning to kill the crabs on the boat turned him into a killer. When at home, he searched out snakes and any other critter he could find to kill. These were mostly snakes, as they were most numerous on the property. We had only lived there a short time, so there was still a lot of brush around the house, and therefore many snakes. Willie had a huge challenge, but he was up to the job.

It was inevitable that an armadillo would eventually try to make a home nearby. It did so under our mobile home. We didn't get much sleep that night due to the barking and growling, but by morning, Willie had the critter dead in the yard, having chewed through its outer shell, thus killing it.

Willie wasn't just a wonderful dog for the two kids, but he was a friend and savior for me. I even took him along fishing a few times when I didn't have far to go. I think he could even understand me at times. I certainly understood him when he was disappointed that he couldn't go in the boat with me.

And Willie was protective of me as well. In fact, Willie saved me from certain harm many times. I remember one morning when I was going fishing, the river was bank-full, and I had my boat pulled well up into the yard. When I got ready to slide my boat back, Willie was at my feet. When I moved the boat, he grabbed a moccasin that was hiding there. It was quite obvious he could smell the snake and was ready to step in when I shoved the boat to expose myself to the danger of getting bitten. Willie took off across the yard with the three-foot snake in his mouth, slinging him as hard as he could. The snake was not able to bite Willie, and the reptile was soon dead. I was much more careful with snakes hiding under my boat from then on, but Willie was always around just in case.

Many of the snakes Willie killed on the property were not venomous, but it was inevitable that he would find the occasional moccasin and get bitten. I remember well, the first time Willie's head swelled up like a basketball. We felt sorry for him and gave him aspirins dissolved in water, but there was little else we could do. In time, however, he recovered and was his usual self again.

He would not leave the snakes alone though. This was his pastime and his job. It was inevitable that snakes would bite him again and again. We didn't know how many times he could take his head swelling up as it did, but there was nothing we could do about it. The snakes would never go away completely.

One day I caught Willie with a snake. It wasn't a venomous variety, but it was six feet long. I don't know who had who, but Willie was running across the yard with a part of the snake in his mouth. That was a sight to see, and I wasn't sure who would win the battle. Finally, the snake got free and slithered into the water. Willie was out of breath and panting hard, but no worse for wear. I don't know if I can say the same for the snake, but I was sure the snake would live. It would remember Willie though.

Snake bites to the face finally got the best of Willie, and though it was forty years ago, I still miss him. He *was* a super dog.

Willie the 'super dog'

Sharing a Hole with a Snake (2016)

Here's another true serpent tale, believe it or not.

My best friend from Fort Worth was down for a few days, and I got him to help me put in a new drain line for the walk-in shower I was installing. The line had to be tied into the existing sewer line underneath the porch decking. I had the deck boards removed, and we dug down to the existing sewer pipe. To connect to the sewer line, the pipe had to be cut; and to do this, all the dirt had to be cleaned from around the pipe.

The hole was about three-feet deep, and my friend was upside down in the hole head-first, cleaning the dirt from around the pipe with a garden tool. I didn't know this at the time, but my buddy had a serious snake phobia. Well, this black snake about three-feet long was apparently sleeping in a cranny underneath the porch, and it decided to slither into the hole.

I had never heard my friend scream like a girl before, but he did that day. I had also never seen him move so fast. When he made it out of the hole, which didn't take but a second or two, he was a much lighter shade of white. Fortunately, the snake was not a lethal species, but instead was a common water snake. It did look a lot like a water moccasin though. It didn't matter what kind of snake it was to Robert. The snake was in his face, and at three-feet long, it was a monster to him.

As soon as my buddy got out of the hole, he grabbed the shovel we used to dig the hole and pinned the reptile to the bottom of the pit. He then began poking the snake with a wild intensity I had never seen him exhibit at anything before. He probably could have killed the snake with the curse words spewing from his mouth. The snake did not suffer, but my best friend will never be the same. He was not bitten or harmed in any way, but that is the last hole he will ever stick his head in.

When it was determined that the snake was in fact not a water moccasin, we both had a good laugh. We laughed for different reasons, however. I laughed at how fast Robert exited the hole backwards, then at his much lighter shade of white. I also laughed at how wildly he flailed the shovel at the snake, and at his long strings of curse words, which continued for some time. He laughed simply because he had survived the ordeal.

When you live in a swamp, there are always critters to deal with, and you just never know when you are going to run into something unexpected. This is reality, but it is still inevitably a little unnerving. My buddy will never be the same, but we are and always will be best friends.

I remember another time when my sister-in-law was visiting. She wanted to go with me to run my trotlines that fine sunny day. The best fishing was not far from the house. My wife decided we'd make a morning of it, and the three of us headed downstream in the boat. The in-laws watched the kids.

My sister-in-law knew how to run and bait the tackle, and wanted to do so for the first few trotlines. She got up in front of the boat from where this task is done. I think it was about the third stop where I had to maneuver under some tree limbs to get to the bank where the trotline was tied. I didn't see the snake in the limb, as I was watching my sister-in-law at the front of the boat to keep her out of the brush. She was watching me when I ducked under the limb, and the snake fell onto my shoulders and slithered down my back. She got a good laugh as I turned a shade of white nearly matching the T-shirt I was wearing.

The snake was not venomous, but just like my best friend, I don't care much for snakes either. I'm not deathly afraid of them, but when they slither down your back or around your feet, it's another story.

My Good Friend Bubba (2009)

One day I decided I needed a scarecrow for my garden, so I dug out an old pair of jeans, and old flannel shirt, and a T-shirt. I found some foam for stuffing and began to sew. When I had the jeans and shirt stuffed and attached to each other, I made a head out of the T-shirt stuffed with more foam and sewed it to the collar of the shirt. I cut a few short pieces off a 2x4 for arms and legs. I stuck the boards into the arms of the shirt and legs of the jeans. I added gloves to the ends of the arms and old sneakers to the ends of the legs. I added an old ball cap, but still, something was missing—the creation needed a face. I got a permanent marker and made eyes with brows, a nose, and a mouth. I also drew ears on each side.

The new scarecrow didn't scare a single bird away from my garden that I could tell. I guess he was just a little too good looking. After all, he looked a lot like me. He was wearing my old clothes, and he was about my size. After the garden was finished, I couldn't toss him in the trash, so I decided to move the fella to the porch. I placed him in my glider, propped his feet up in a chair, and placed his arms in a leisurely position. Up to this point, I had not named the scarecrow, but finally decided that Bubba was a fitting moniker.

Bubba remained on the back porch for a few years, and I talked to him frequently every time I crossed his path. He became a friendly face after my divorce. He always had a smile, and I never heard a cross word from him. I lived alone during this time, and he was a good listener.

There came a time when I no longer needed Bubba to keep me company. This was after I met Ellen. One Halloween I decided to string Bubba up in front of the house. I got a rope and a folding chair and took Bubba to the front driveway. A few days before Halloween, I placed Bubba where he could easily be seen from the road into the property. I placed him in the center of the driveway to look as if he had hanged himself.

Out here in the country, not many people would see Bubba, but as luck would have it, a group of illegal aliens happened along late one night with cops in tow. After the cops had rounded up most of the illegals, the paddy wagon arrived and loaded up the men and women to take them to the local county lockdown. The female cop driving the paddy wagon used my driveway to turn around, and when she did, her headlights shined on Bubba, and she saw him hanging from a tree. I got a good laugh out of that. I talked to her a couple of years later, and she still remembered me well, due to her encounter with Bubba. Bubba is still a vibrant memory for me, and a household name around here.

Bubba

Babies! (2016)

Gophers are not generally a problem in the swamp, but with the drought over the past five years or so, things changed. We are coming out of the drought now, but gophers remain. I have been fighting the critters in my orchard and around the house for years, yet they persist.

Today I was digging out a gopher hole in an attempt to eradicate the pest. To my surprise, the nest didn't seem to go anywhere. There are usually tunnels running underground over a large area. This nest, however, was different. It didn't take long to find out why.

Last week I found some white shell-like pieces on the ground in another area. I didn't know what they were. I do now. They're egg shells. As I continued to dig into what I thought was a gopher hole, I found a baby turtle. Then another and another. I found a total of nine babies. In with them were the same white shell-like pieces I found in the other area of the yard previously.

The babies were snapping turtles, which are common around here. I have them in my ponds and shoot them regularly. They are another pest. More of a nuisance really, than a pest. They dig holes in the yard, they stink, and there are so many it seems. My best friend from the north thinks they are good eating—maybe when the apocalypse hits.

It's easy to kill adult turtles, but babies are a different story. They were so cute. I didn't release them into my pond, but I did turn them loose on the riverbank at the water's edge. They immediately scurried into the water, but most hung around a while as they got used to the river. They seemed quite happy the short time they stayed, but soon they were gone. Maybe I'll think twice about shooting one next time. I'm getting soft in my old age. Bah! lol

Baby turtles

War in the Swamp (2016)

There is one thing for certain when you live in a swamp: you will always be at war with something. This time it's gophers. For the first time in two years, however, I am winning the war. Due to the recent drought, gophers showed up here and multiplied rapidly. When I first noticed them, there were already several mounds and likely an extended family of the pests.

I tried using gassers and baits for two years to eradicate the pests to no avail. In order to kill a gopher with baits, the varmint has to eat the stuff. When they're digging and pushing dirt, they often cover up the bait in the process, so they don't eat the poison and therefore don't die. The trenches and damage continue.

With gassers, the deadly vapor must penetrate all the tunnels to kill the pests reliably. There may be as many as eight tunnels for the gas to fill, and gophers can easily block the poison with dirt in a matter of seconds, thus rendering the method ineffective.

The only way you can tell if you've actually killed the gophers with baits and gassers is that they stop trenching and piling up mounds of dirt. For two years, the dirt kept piling up, and the gophers expanded their territory over most of my yard. Gassers and baits may have killed a few, but they continued to gain ground.

Finally, a new solution—cinch traps. Why are these the perfect solution? First, they seem to work every time. The traps are easy to set and when tripped the result is a dead gopher. You have the dead varmint as evidence of the kill. When you open a gopher hole to set the trap, the pest will always try to close the hole back up. The result is one less pest. The gophers don't get sick from ingesting small amounts of poison, and they don't get sick from inhaling small amounts of noxious gasses; instead they die quickly and as humanely as possible. This really isn't that important to me, but I thought I'd mention it for those of you to whom it does matter. See, I care about others. Maybe not as much as some would like, but yes, I do care.

I caught three gophers the first afternoon in a matter of just a few hours, one the next morning, and another two days later. I caught a sixth starting a new hole the following day, and he is history as well. It's been over a week and there is no fresh digging. In less than a week and a lot less of my valuable time spent, all the gophers appear to be gone. Even if they are not, I have the traps, and there will be no extra expense to solve the problem quickly and effectively. After two weeks, there were no more mounds anywhere in the yard. I concluded that I had won the battle. As always, however, there will be other battles to fight. That is the way of the swamp.

What's That in the Air Conditioner Condenser? (2013)

First of all, let me explain what an A/C condenser unit is for those of you who don't know. It is the big part of the air-conditioning system, which sits outside. It contains the compressor, which compresses the Freon coolant, and the fan motor and coils to chill the coolant. That's what makes your A/C work. The inside unit merely moves the air through your home.

Now, to my story.

One day I noticed my A/C was not cooling properly. I had installed the unit, but no longer worked on them. I could have, but I didn't want to anymore. So, I called an A/C buddy of mine with whom I had worked years before when I was a contractor. I knew he would fix the problem and do me right on price. He certainly did this.

While he had the condensing unit open on top, I noticed a considerable amount of leaves and twigs inside the enclosure. The top is an open grille, and after a couple of years, leaves and other trash accumulate inside the unit. Over time, this can deteriorate the coils at the bottom due to excessive moisture, and if enough trash gets inside, it can restrict flow through the coils and therefore reduce the efficiency of the unit.

Well! I decided to reach in and pull some of the leaves out. To my surprise, the very first handful of leaves had a small copperhead snake in it.

By the time I saw the snake, he, it, or whatever you want to call it, clamped down on my hand where my thumb is attached to the palm. It didn't take me long to look at the snake, and I immediately threw it to the ground and began to dance on its head and every other part of it. For once, I had shoes on, which is rare for me around here when it is warm or reasonably so. The little snake died quickly, to say the least.

I looked at where the snake had bitten me. I could see a thin line of blood where luckily only one fang went into my skin. My blood filled the puncture made by the fang, but not enough that the wound would bleed. I squeezed on the area trying to get the venom out. It still didn't bleed, as the snake and therefore its fangs were very small. I didn't get any of the venom out either.

Since the snake was very young and I slung the critter to the ground very quickly, it didn't get much venom into me, but I was certain I got some. From what I am told, baby venom is more potent than the venom of older snakes; therefore it doesn't take as much to hurt you. I decided I needed some medication to help counteract any effects the venom might have. I decided on ibuprofen and Benadryl.

It was a couple of hours before I felt any ill effects. I was nauseated at first, but there was almost no pain. It felt much like getting bitten by a mosquito, which is a daily occurrence here in the swamp during warmer weather. This is most of the year.

I did not appear to run a fever because of the venom, but I did have a slight headache and felt a bit sick to my stomach for a couple of days. Then this eased off and I was good as new. Just another day in the swamp!

You Just Never Know... A Fishing Story! (2016)

On Sunday May 29, 2016, Ellen and I made a fishing trip upstream from the house. Since the river was high, I decided there had to be fish moving up to the spawning areas. We stopped at several locations that looked good and got a few bites, but no fish. Finally, further up Ellen caught a nice catfish. I continued to get a few bites, but could not catch anything. The fish were apparently small and were just stealing my bait. We refer to these fish collectively as 'bait-stealers'.

We were using shrimp for bait, and I was certain there would be fish to be caught, but still, Ellen had caught the only one. It was a nice catch, but I thought there should be more. Then, I spilled my Big Red® soda on the boat seat and onto my baited hook. No big deal, and I cast my line back out. Quickly, I caught a nice fish. *Hmm*, I thought. I re-baited my hook, and this time I dipped my shrimp into the Big Red®, which was still in a puddle on the boat seat. I immediately caught a second fish. I repeated the process and caught a third. *They must be liking the Big Red®!* I thought. Ellen wanted some soda for her bait too.

I did it a fourth time, but there were no fish to be caught. I must have caught the last of them, because if there had been another, it would have certainly bitten the shrimp laced with soda. We decided to call it a day and went home. I caught the three on soda-dunked shrimp, and Ellen caught two, the second using the soda-dunking technique. She actually caught a third, but it was on the small side, and she released it to grow a bit and catch another day.

I am reasonably certain the soda had nothing to do with me catching the three fish, but you just never know. The next time I'm not catching anything, maybe I'll just add a little Big Red® to the bait. Ellen has decided this was a good idea. Since then, she uses some of my Big Red® all the time. I use it occasionally too when Ellen seems to be catching more fish than I am. If something's not working, try something different. This is a good rule to remember.

Before Today She Could Only Imagine the Excitement! (2017)

I have taken Ellen fishing many times over the past year, but one particular day was special. She moved to my swamp nearly two years ago, along the Guadalupe River on the Texas Gulf Coast. Never having the opportunity to go fishing anytime she wanted, Ellen and I now go nearly every week. It was Mother's Day, and she wanted to go. The weather was perfect, and she was in the mood. It was a no-brainer.

We headed upstream, and I picked what looked like a good spot. Ellen got her line in the water and on the first cast she caught a nice blue cat. I gave her a smile and a high-five. She almost immediately caught the second fish.

I had fished this river most of my life and caught more fish than I could count. I told Ellen many stories about 'pole benders', and while the fish she caught had been legal and fun for her to catch, the largest only weighed about five pounds. Those are good eating size, but none were what I considered large.

After Ellen caught eight or so fish while I had caught only two, she hooked into yet another one. She yanked hard on her rod and started to reel it in, but when the line tightened up, her pole bent sharply, and the line stopped. It wouldn't budge.

"I'm hung up," she said, disappointed.

We have a lot of logs and branches in our river, so getting hung up happens fairly often. If it's a bad snag, it usually means you need to cut your line and re-do your tackle.

Ellen pulled hard and held a strain on the line, but it was definitely stuck. She let some line spool off, hoping the current would carry the line downstream and pull her off the log. A few moments later, she tried to reel the line in again—it was still stuck. But wait! The snag didn't seem to be in the same spot as before! Then it started moving slowly upstream!

As she held the line taut, the log was moving against the current. How was this possible? With her rod doubled over, we realized that was no log. She had hooked into a monster! I had the dip net ready, but the creature did not surface as it passed by the boat and continued away from us. Her pole bent even more, line pulled against the drag, and started spooling off the reel.

"It's gigantic! It's going to break my pole," she yelled, her eyes popping wide open and her mouth gaping. "Help me!!"

I told her I couldn't do anything better than what she was doing.

She held on for dear life as whatever she had on the end of her line turned and headed downstream, strong and steady. It was just going. This fish was unstoppable.

Suddenly, the line went slack. Ellen reeled it in. The hook and sinker were still attached, but the fish got away. We would like to have seen what she tangled with, but that would be a mystery forever. There were really only two things it could have been. From my experience fishing the river, I am guessing it was a large yellow cat, also known as a flathead catfish. The other option is a gar. We had seen some large gar all morning, but to me, it didn't quite act like one. I'm still guessing it was a 40- to 50-pound catfish.

15-pound yellow cat (aka flathead catfish)

Though Ellen did not land the fish, she did get to feel the power of what I call a 'pole bender'. The excitement was like no other she had ever felt. One day, she will get the chance to feel the awesome power of a big monster once again. I can't wait for the day I see that look on her face one more time. Maybe next time we'll at least get to see what it is, and just maybe, she can land it. Experiences like this are worth their weight in gold.

A Leisurely Stroll Around Outside (2016)

Ellen had foot surgery a week and a half ago. She has a little stroller for her leg, so she is mobile, but the scooter does not do well on rough terrain, so we made a short trip around the house on the paved road. Ellen felt she needed more exercise and requested the walkabout.

About halfway through the trip, she heard a sound in the grass and weeds. I told her it was a frog, but when I went into the nearly knee-high weeds, it began to sound like something other than what I had said it was. It sounded like something was hurt, and I couldn't see the critter. I pulled some of the weeds and vines away to try to see what it was. Maybe a snake with a mouse in its mouth. I really didn't know at this point.

I decided it really didn't matter and Ellen wanted to continue her walk back to the house, so we left the critter, whatever it was, alone. It was a beautiful day, and our minds drifted off to better things as we gazed at the garden, flowers, and bright blue sky. Ellen and I both love flowers, and I grow a good many crepe myrtle, Esperanza, and Pride of Barbados plants.

My crepe myrtle; My Esperanza

My Pride of Barbados

When we got back to the house, Ellen went about her business and me, mine. Shortly, my best friend called to talk a while, and I sat on the porch. One of the stories I told him was the encounter with the noise and elusive critter or critters in the weeds. He asked me if I was tromping around in the weeds with shoes in case the animal was dangerous. "No!" I replied rather indignant. "I don't wear shoes." My buddy got a big laugh out of this, and that's when he suggested I write another tale about the incident. Now you know why I wrote this story.

I can't imagine why he thought the fact I wasn't wearing shoes was so funny. I never wear shoes unless I'm going to town or it's too cold to go barefoot. That's not often here in south Texas. I was born barefoot and spent much of my childhood barefoot. They made me wear shoes in the third grade, but I soon acquired a pair of moccasins, which were as close to barefoot as I could get and still keep the adults happy.

I wore shoes, boots, and other footwear much of my life because of my work, but now that I am retired and don't have to answer to anyone else, I choose to go without shoes, so guess what I'm wearing right now? Right—nothing.

Our Wild Sex Life (2017)

We're doing the best that we can.

What? You expected more? lol

Peaceful Valley (2016)

When Ellen read this story, she said our valley didn't feel like a valley at all. I told her there is a 30-foot high bluff to the west and another to the northeast. I assured her we live in a valley. The gorge is four-miles wide and flat, but it's still a valley. She frowned.

Life is about change—some is good; other is not. But one thing is certain; nothing lasts forever. There will be change soon because life in the valley has been very quiet and peaceful. But whatever happens, I will always love my little valley. It is springtime, and the garden is growing well. There have been plenty of fish to catch, and the weather is very pleasant. Temperatures in the swamp have been 60's for lows and middle 70's for highs. What more could anyone ask for?

A couple of turkeys wandered through the yard yesterday. They were mature females and didn't stay around long, but they were delightful to see. The ducks and geese will be gone soon, and I'll miss hearing and seeing them. A couple

Mallard duck wants a little corn

of wild ducks have been feeding in the pond next to the house, and a mallard I raised a couple of years ago has been hanging around the past few weeks. He visits several times a year. I wonder if he'll migrate north this year. He stays gone for months at a time, but then he shows up for a visit. He likes the corn I feed him. He pecks at the door to let me know he's hungry.

I'd like to share a few photos I took today, as I am always snapping a picture or two around the place. The first two show Texas Evening Primrose and the new peaches, which are growing well this year. The next shows how primrose decorates my yard. The last one is a photo of my Spring garden.

Texas Evening Primrose; Early yellow peaches

My extended yard with Texas Evening Primrose

My Spring garden

The potatoes are doing well, and the corn is coming along. Beets and beans are getting started along with some winter carrots. The peanuts are just coming up, and I have cantaloupe started in small pots, which I'll plant out into the garden soon. This will be the bulk of what I grow this year. Ellen grows her stuff in her separate garden. These include tomatoes, cucumbers, peas, squash, Brussels sprouts, broccoli, and herbs.

There's nothing like fresh vegetables from the garden. I like the corn, potatoes, beets, and green beans mostly, but I'll eat some from Ellen's garden. You can't imagine how much better stuff tastes when it's fresh. We grow a lot, and there is always excess to give away. It's good practice in case the grid shuts down, and we're forced to provide for ourselves. You would know why this is important if you have read *Into Autumn*, book one in my series. You can find it at all book retailers, including Amazon.

Life is Great When It's Uneventful! (2016)

No matter where you live, no matter what you do, no matter who you are, sometimes there is absolutely nothing happening in life. Don't let that bore you though. Life is all in how you look at it.

Around here in the swamp, uneventful is what you want life to be. If something is happening, it's usually something crazy like flooding, snakes, alligators, and so many other things to deal with that it's not even funny.

A nothing day is okay for me because Ellen and I can take a pleasant walk down the road behind the house. There, we can watch wispy clouds in the sky, and the birds, and we can listen to the sounds they make, which are always pleasing to the ear. Woodpeckers are numerous, as are doves of several varieties. In fact, there are about as many different varieties of birds in and around my swamp as there are anywhere else in the USA. The Audubon Society conducts bird counts regularly around here, and the varieties we have are well-documented. Birdwatchers come around often too.

Imagine a slow, peaceful stroll in the countryside with a little breeze in your face and warm sunshine on your back. No mosquitos, no cars, no city noise, just the rustle of tree leaves and an occasional whistle as a mourning dove flies out of a nearby tree, spooked by our presence.

We have time to think without interruption, and for a little meaningful conversation as we stroll along hand-in-hand. What could be nicer than that?

So, the next time you think you want to be buzzing down the highway at 80 mph with the radio blaring, window shopping on a city street, or even reading a fast-paced book as quickly as your eyes will take you from page to page, think about me, taking a leisurely stroll in the peace and quiet of my swamp.

Shhh! I'll be quiet for a few minutes while you take a look at a few photos I've compiled especially for you:

My young ducklings

My nearly grown ducks

A young deer passing through

Relaxing, fishing on the Guadalupe River

Me and Dandy, my pet deer

Fresh shrimp for bait, and a squid

An unwelcome visitor

Our road behind the house

A hawk passing through

My Fall garden

Peaches ripening

Softshell turtle

Water in the back yard

Me and a couple of nice catfish

My ducks on a pond

Ellen caught an eel

The Day My World Blew Up in My Face, Literally! (2000)

This is the one story that does not actually take place in or near my swamp. It takes place in Palacios, Texas. I have nearly died several times during my life, but this was the worst. This incident was a life-changer. It made me appreciate my swamp more and showed me I had better enjoy every day to its fullest. You never know when your last day on earth will come. This day came very close to being my final moment.

It was December 8, 2000, and I had just picked up Ernest, my helper for the day. I was a contractor working on a roofing job in Palacios, Texas. On the way to the jobsite, we stopped by a local propane company in Port Lavaca to fill the 10-gallon propane tank for melting and sealing the thermoplastic membrane we used to waterproof the roof.

When we arrived at the jobsite at 8:00 a.m., Ernest set up the ladder and began to carry tools and supplies onto the top of the building. I secured the ladder behind him, took the freshly filled propane tank up, and set it in the middle of the roof. Ernest and I started installing the metal trim around the perimeter of the building, as the roof surface had already been completed. It was time to finish the perimeter waterproofing.

After we had installed several pieces of trim, Ernest continued to install the trim, while I went to get started heating the thermoplastic membrane strips to seal them to the metal and the roof along the perimeter. I grabbed several membrane strips and took them over to the edge of the roof, then returned for the torch and propane tank. I walked up to grab the tank, and when I touched it, it exploded.

The next thing I knew, I was lying on my back about ten feet from where the tank exploded, watching a cloud of propane vapor rising high into the air. I was knocked out instantly, but only for a few seconds. I was numb. I knew I was hurt severely. I touched my mid-section, and it felt cold. Liquid propane is about -50 degrees and I was splashed with it. There was almost no blood, but I knew it had to be bad.

Ernest was some distance away and was unhurt by the blast, but it scared him enough that he jumped off the ten-foot-high roof to get help. A woman in a house across the street came out after hearing the explosion. She asked Ernest if we needed help, then she went back inside and made the call to 911.

The EMS station was about a mile down the road. They arrived quickly and began to assess my situation. One of the men said they had heard the explosion and began to get their gear ready as they waited for the call. They said they knew someone had to have been hurt by the intensity of the bang.

As one of the technicians examined me, the other two, along with Ernest, set up another ladder. They got their transfer cage to the roof and placed me in it. The men slid me down the two ladders crossways, loaded me onto a gurney, then put me into the back of the ambulance.

The trip to the hospital seemed to take forever. There was no hospital in the fishing community where the accident occurred. I was taken to Bay City about fifty miles away. I could feel every little bump, and there were many. As the minutes passed, I could feel the numbness going away, and the pain was nearly unbearable by the time we reached the emergency entrance. I began to fade out.

It seemed like only seconds until I reached the operating room where three surgeons were waiting. They were ready when I arrived. The anesthesiologist told me to count backwards from a hundred. I recall getting to ninety-seven.

I awoke in a bed. I was alive. I had monitors and tubes hooked up in every place where something could be hooked up. And I hurt.

My pelvis was not only fractured in several places; it was broken in half. The explosion ripped my stomach open from hip to hip. Both legs were ripped open on the inside near the femoral artery. My backbone was also severely aggravated. My bladder exploded from the impact. One of my testicles was ripped out and destroyed beyond repair. The tissues around the entire area had been damaged significantly due to the trauma. Much of the area was hard like concrete. It was one very large dried blood clot. It's no wonder I very nearly died.

I don't remember a lot about the next few days. I was drugged heavily. I remember eating a little once or twice, and nurses were constantly fiddling with me. Every time I would doze off, someone would wake me back up to check my vitals and give me pills.

Day four, I was still alive, and the hospital staff moved me to a private room. The nurses gave me a small amount of food under the doctor's orders. The hospital food actually tasted good. I was still in a lot of pain and the morphine, for which I had a control switch, only took the edge off the agony. It never subsided completely.

My surgeon came in every day and made changes to the nurse's routine and medications. It was shortly after I was moved into the private room when the doctor decided my intestines had shut down. He also found a bright yellow liquid staining my bedclothes and called in the urologist who had helped put me back together in the operating room. The yellow liquid was not urine. I overheard the doctor tell one of the nurses my intestines needed to be stimulated, or they might begin dying. This would necessitate more surgery.

I was also bloated from the food my body could not process. A nurse inserted a tube down my throat, and I remember three things. First, was the nastiest and vilest liquid that gushed into the container, which fortunately was mostly sealed.

Second, I remember the huge relief when the pressure was released. I felt like I was going to explode, like a balloon about to pop. The relief was welcome.

Third, I felt extremely hungry. I was always hungry, but it's hard to eat on a full stomach. Now that my stomach had been emptied, I wanted to eat, but my intestines were shut down. No one was going to give me food at this point. The tube was left in my stomach, and a pump added. The nurses continually pumped my stomach for several days.

I remember the mention of at least three types of enemas, but the one that sticks in my mind is the 'slushy' enema. They cut off all food for four days while my intestines were stimulated. I ate a total of one cup of crushed ice over those four days. I wasn't going to die of starvation because of the IV, but I was getting damn hungry.

Another problem was that every time the nurses had to change the bed pads, the pain shot through my body to the point of nearly passing out. I asked for a trapeze bed, so I could lift myself straight up to allow the nurses to change the dirty pad. The twisting was what was killing me when the two halves of my pelvis ground together. Even in my weakened condition, I was still strong enough to hold my body weight up long enough for this task to be completed. The trapeze was a welcome addition.

My doctor ordered another CT scan to take a second look at my injuries. Again, the twisting and moving from the bed to the gurney, a flat and cold board slid underneath me, and then onto the CT scan table shot excruciating pain through my body. Then the procedure was reversed with an equal, if not more severe, amount of pain.

Finally, my intestines started working on the eighth day, and I made a big mess in the bed. I apologized to the nurses, but they took it in stride and with a smile. I don't think I could have done that. Nurses everywhere have my respect.

At one point, the doctor prescribed some medication that made me hallucinate badly. The dream continued for two nights and was the same both nights. I dreamt that I had to roll twine into a ball. As the ball got bigger and bigger, the ball became impossible to manage, yet I couldn't stop. I woke up screaming in frustration of not being able to continue with my task.

Ernest came to visit when I was able to talk to him; probably on the 4th or 5th day. He had some questions about what I wanted to do about the roof we were working on. I asked him to do whatever he needed to do to complete the job and keep track of his hours. I gave him full use of my truck to get the job done. He completed the perimeter with flashing cement and coated the roof to finish the job.

On the ninth day, my doctor came in and checked me out. That was the first time I remember actually looking at my injuries. There was a row of metal staples about eight inches long between my navel and groin area. It looked nasty. The tissues on my legs and stomach had solidified into a giant blood clot. I lay my head back down. I didn't want to see any more.

Now that my intestines were working again, and I seemed to be doing better, my doctor commented that he really had thought I was going to die. The morphine was finally doing its job to my satisfaction. My doctor called a therapist in to get me walking, and it was she who gave me my first real shower in over a week. I had been up and down a few times, but the farthest I'd walked was to the toilet, the door, and to the chair in the room.

I don't remember her name now, but she was a tiny gal. She assured me she would not let me fall. With the help of a walker, her holding onto me tightly with a strap high around my waist, she helped me into the shower and removed my hospital gown. She scrubbed me without saying a word and cleaned every square inch of my body. I fell in love with her at once. The warm water felt so good against my body! And when she cleaned my private parts I began to feel alive again. There was no way there would be any reaction she would notice, though I felt the blood stirring.

The doctor also put me back on food again, starting with a liquid diet. That day I had the best meal I have ever had in my entire life. It was only beef broth, but after not eating for so many days, it tasted better than any steak I had ever eaten, and I do love a good ribeye.

I got hungry several nights, and at this point, I couldn't seem to get enough food. The liquid diet wasn't staying with me very long, and I talked one of the night nurses into sneaking me some popsicles. They were wonderful.

This little therapist gal came in every day, and we walked to the door and back at first. Then we made the trek into the hallway and finally down to the end of the hall after the third day. I say we walked, but with my walker and my pretty therapist holding onto me not so tightly now, I managed to scoot my feet along to make my way down the corridor.

By the 12th day, my doctor decided there was no more that he or the hospital could do for me. I could go home. I didn't feel I was ready and chose to stay an extra day. I still didn't feel strong enough, but went home anyway.

A few days after getting home, a physical therapist began coming in twice a week. I was pretty much healed up, but I was a long way away from being well. I could not walk without a walker, could not get out of bed without assistance, and though I ate plenty, I didn't seem to have any strength except in my upper body. I had worked hard all my life and was very strong because of the work, but the only strength I had now was in my upper half. The bottom half seemed all but dead.

My intestines were not only working again; they were working overtime. I had a lot of digestive problems. I could not eat anything that was remotely spicy or hard to digest. And the food was going through me like there was no tomorrow. A good friend suggested chlorophyll tablets. I took his advice. He suggested taking about a dozen at a time. They weren't going to hurt me and just might do me some good.

I took a batch of the pills twice, but they didn't work. I pooped them out undissolved in two hours. They didn't have a chance to help me. They went through my body so fast most of them wouldn't even dissolve. My thought was that maybe the food was also going through me so fast that my body couldn't absorb enough nutrients to nourish me. I thought this might also be the reason I was so hungry all the time, regardless of how much I ate, which was a lot.

I went back to the doctor. He prescribed a little fast dissolving pill, which taken over a month, slowed my intestines down to a more normal rate. That did the trick.

I have been a survivor all my life by necessity. I wasn't going to let this get me down. I would get stronger. I would do whatever I needed to do to get back into shape. I did the exercises my therapist instructed me to do. I was in constant pain, but I did the work. Often, walking only consisted of a walk to the bathroom, then around the kitchen/living room.

In between my exercise sessions, there was very little else I could do. This gave me plenty of time to think—to realize how lucky I was. If the top half of the propane tank, which hit me just above the groin when the tank separated in the middle, had hit me anywhere else, I'd have died. If the propane had ignited, I'd have died. If the lacerations on the inside of my legs had reached an artery, which they barely missed, I'd have died. There were so many other 'what ifs' that could have easily resulted in my death. But they didn't.

I was so lucky, despite how bad the incident was. Accidents over which you have no control can happen at any time, and they will happen in an instant. This got me to thinking. I was strong enough to survive something like this. My life of hard manual labor saved me. You only live once, and I very nearly lost it all.

Now, if I am going to die, I will have lived as well as I can. This experience mellowed me considerably and changed my life forever, for the better. Someone once said, "Only you can make you happy." I truly believe that. If you are not happy, you have the power to make your life better. Do whatever you need to do to be happy. Don't let anything stand in your way. You only have one chance at life, and if you are not happy, you're wasting it. You never know when fate is going to blow up in your face.

Weeks with my physical therapist got me to where I could stand, lift a foot off the floor, and walk. I still needed the walker, but I was walking more than scooting now. I was going outside too. It was January, and I really don't remember it being all that cold, but I was eating a lot and exercising too—my body was generating an enormous amount of heat, so I didn't get cold, even dressed lightly.

I walked out to the mailbox, which was normally a one-minute or less stroll. That took fifteen minutes. I was moving along! I practiced getting in and out of my truck unassisted. Good thing there was a grab handle just inside the door. I wouldn't have made it without it.

My son-in-law needed a new job, and I needed someone to take care of the working end of my contracting business. After I was able to drive my truck safely, I started going to the jobsites to check on his work. I gave up my walker for a cane. Climbing the ladder was good exercise. I was intent on getting back to my old self—the tough SOB I once was. And maybe, just maybe, not so much of the SOB I had always been.

A year later, I could do light work. Two years later, I could do moderate work, but not nearly enough hard work to return to my business. So, I decided it was time for me to retire. My lawyers had a field day with the people who filled the propane tank, the manufacturers of the propane tank and the pop-off valve which didn't pop off to relieve the pressure in the tank. So, I retired. Over time, my son-in-law couldn't handle the work, or at least couldn't make me any money, so I eventually shut the company down.

I did finally return to doing some small jobs from time to time to supplement my income. A couple of years ago, I decided I just didn't have to do the work anymore and really retired. But a person like me retiring is nothing like it is for most people I suspect. I imagine most people retire to a life of leisure. That may or may not be the actual truth of the matter, but I certainly will never have a sedentary life. I maintain nine acres with an orchard of about 80 fruit trees of all kinds, and a large garden, and I'm constantly doing a re-model around the house. I'm also fighting critters of all sorts, large and small. Maybe my biggest job now is taking care of Ellen, though this gives me a lot of pleasure and satisfaction as well. It's my primary job, but it's no chore.

I found I like flying. I started flying a couple of years before I met Ellen. Love of travel is one of the main things we have in common. Las Vegas is my favorite destination, but Ellen and I have traveled to several exotic locations, as well as numerous areas of the continental USA, Alaska, and Hawaii.

Travel makes Ellen happy, and it makes me happy, so we do it. Like I said earlier, if you are not happy, it's your own fault. You only live once, so live life to its fullest. You will die one day, and you never know when that might be. You may as well die knowing you got all you could get out of life.

Dangers of the Deep (1975)

One of the many dangers in my swamp doesn't involve critters at all. A boat and motor are a necessity when you live on a river. If you spend enough time motoring up and down the river, sooner or later you're going to hit a stump.

One day I was fishing in South River, a lower section of the Guadalupe near the bay. I was scooting along at about fifteen miles per hour and hit a submerged stump. I didn't just graze it as is often the case; I hit it dead center.

The motor immediately flipped up out of the water, the force of the stump turned the boat toward the shore, and it jumped up on the bank as my body slammed into the floor boards.

Buzzing down the river in my flat-bottom boat

I didn't get hurt, but the event was certainly a shock. I rose up and looked back toward the transom (rear end of the boat), but the motor wasn't there. Fortunately for me, however, it had an electric start and had electrical wires connected to a battery. Otherwise, I would have lost the motor. I grabbed the cables and pulled the submerged motor out of the water and into the boat. I then re-attached it to the transom and tightened it down.

I immediately pulled the cowling off the motor and pulled the plugs out. I hit the electric start and forced the water out of the cylinders. I then re-installed the plugs and pumped the gas bulb, forcing fresh gas into the system, then hit the starter again. The motor started right up. I slid the boat off the bank, and went on my way. An incident like that sticks with you. I remembered where that stump was for a long, long time.

Who's to Blame... Our Dying Estuary? (2017)

It started a long time ago. I don't know who's to blame, but somebody is. Will they tell? Not on your life! I do like to rant from time to time, but I have tried not to do so in this book. This story will be my exception.

The swamp is not what it used to be and never will be again. The forces of evil are at work, and there is nothing you and I can do about it. The main government agency responsible for preserving my swamp is the Texas Parks and Wildlife Department (TP&WD), and they are busy doing everything they can to destroy it. They aren't the only agency involved.

The Guadalupe-Blanco River Authority is involved too, and I suspect there are a few other agencies whom collectively I'll call the Department of Evil—The Natural Resource Conservation Service, the Department of Agriculture, and the Environmental Protection Agency. Who knows who else?

They are not doing this destructive act on purpose, but rather the destruction is a side-effect of their plan to create their own special world for sportsmen's benefit to the detriment of anyone or anything standing in their way. The Plan is the result of overpopulation, the root cause of most problems on this planet.

The TP&WD was slammed financially for damaging private property owned by local men a few years back, but this hasn't seemed to deter their efforts.

For much of my life, I have been in their way, and I have suffered as a result. That is all I will say with respect to this. I fought them a few times, and I lost. I already wrote that book, *Dangerous Waters* (1986), which is now out of print. Only the money of a Trump, Gates, or Carnegie could fight them. My primary focus will be on the effects of their efforts.

The abundance of black moss and clams, which are a source of food for catfish, has deteriorated significantly. The government has built levies and dams which alter the flow of water into the estuary. They've used chemicals to control aquatic plants to protect the interests of some, at the expense of others and the natural resources we eat. What is this doing to my health?

And what's with the gaspergou (drum) and piranha? Only since Ellen moved to the river have I seen any freshwater drum in these waters. They are common in Louisiana, but are a new species here. I have no idea how puku piranha got into the Guadalupe River. My step-dad caught two of the toothy critters. I guess it really doesn't matter much anymore. People don't swim in this area as we did so often when I was growing up, but they will eventually affect other living things. The alligator gar is probably more of a danger to swimmers anyway. I remember one of my cousins getting bitten back in the sixties as she swam in the river. Too many gar will also affect other animals.

Boosting the population significantly of one or two species of creatures will have the equal and opposite effect on the other species who share the same environment. Some of the critters which have been intentionally boosted by one means or another have been alligators, redfish (red drum), and buffalo fish. As a result, catfish, shrimp, crabs, and a few other less significant varieties have suffered.

When you boost a species, what they eat will decline, and if they share the same breeding space, over-crowding occurs to the harm of the lesser plants and animals. This is common sense, but the plan must prevail. The TP&WD also performs sampling of the many species, distorts their results to justify their plan, and the damage continues. They are a highly visible government agency, have big bucks behind them, and they know what they are doing! Why? Because they are a government agency? Bullshit! But the general public is probably 90% plus behind them. Why? Ignorance for one. Indifference for another.

This process of destruction started decades ago when I was a commercial fisherman. An additional destructive process by our government was the insertion of hordes of Vietnamese fishermen into the shrimping industry. This resulted in extensive over-fishing of many species—shrimp, crabs, and oysters. All the forces of evil resulted in my demise as a commercial fisherman, and I have been bitter as a result ever since.

Nature is now fighting back to some extent it seems, and I am at least happy about that. I will continue to do what I can to help the one species I can actually do something about, and that is catfish. For the present, there are more catfish than I have seen in a couple of decades, but the numbers are only a small fraction of what they were back in the sixties and seventies. That is a shame, but at least we are eating catfish regularly.

I guess none of this really matters. We, as a whole, are killing this planet anyway. It will not likely affect me, but one day our kids, grandkids, or future

Gaspergou (freshwater drum)

Puku piranha

generations are going to be faced with a calamity like no one has ever seen. The world will change, and people will die in droves. That is something you can wager on, but you'll never get paid off. It is sad, but after the humans infesting this planet are mostly dead and gone, the world will heal and start over. Hopefully, humans will not make the same mistakes the second time around.

Thank you for putting up with my rant. Now, how about a nail-biting tale from my swamp?

That Son-of-a-bitch Harvey Almost Got the Best of Me (2017)

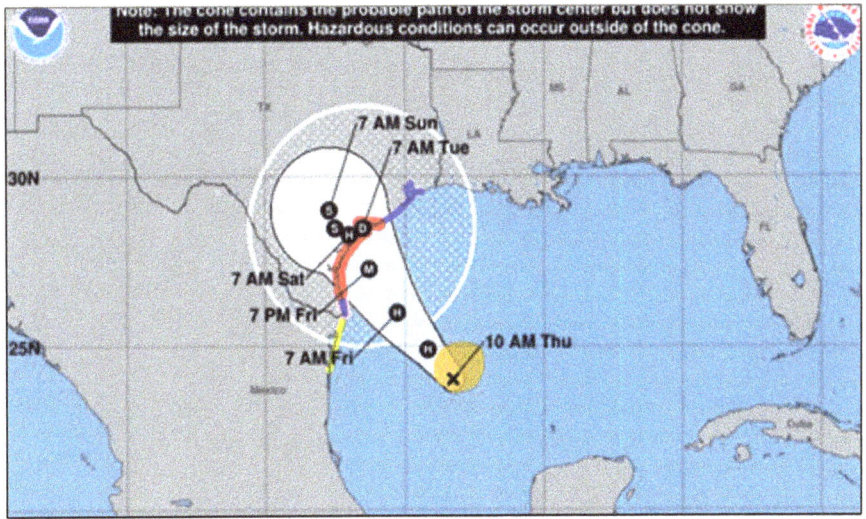

Hurricane Harvey waltzes into my place

It's 2:30 a.m. on August 26, 2017, and here I squat on the tool-box of my truck holding onto the ladder rack for my life. The water level is up to the tool-box, and three-foot waves are crashing into my back, driven by 140 mph winds. Hurricane Harvey is at its peak now, just coming on shore. I'm on the nasty side of the storm, the right front quadrant, and the outer edge of Harvey's eyewall band is lashing at me with all his fury.

Heavy rain is pelting my backside, cold and stinging my skin even through my shirt, alternating with warm waves breaking onto me and into the side of the truck. Debris carried by the water is hitting me in the back and head often. A constant stream of water runs down my face, and the scream of the wind drowns out all other sounds. There is nothing I can do but hope this will all work out for the best.

An hour earlier, I was trying to sleep in the hallway, the strongest area of my home. I reset my alarm every thirty minutes so I could check the water level outside. At 1:30 a.m. there was no water in the yard other than a small puddle from the rain. At 2:00, five feet of water and waves lashed at the side of my house.

I had no fear of 140 mph winds blowing my home down. I built it with my own two hands and made certain it would stand up to any hurricane. I had no fear of rising water because I built the house to take flood waters, but what I did fear was the waves hitting the outside wall. Tons and tons of water slamming against the wall could, and I feared would, take the wall down much like having your feet kicked out from underneath you. I did not know how much higher the water would rise, but even a couple of feet could collapse the wall—the place would fall like a house of cards, and I would most surely die. That is what I thought was going to happen. So, I decided to leave.

I grabbed a duffle bag, quickly threw some clothes in, stuck my phone in my pocket, picked up a portable LED light, and made my way to my truck parked in the driveway. I cranked her up and turned on the headlights. The water was halfway up the driveway, and I headed to the road towards the main highway and higher ground. I have been through many floods over the years, and the water had never been up to the Guadalupe River bridge on Hwy 35. I figured I would park and ride out the rest of the storm there.

I estimated the water on my roadway to be about one and a half feet deep and saw that I would be driving downwind to the highway and safety. No problem, I imagined, as my truck had a diesel engine and could take deeper water than if it had a gasoline engine. I had driven through more than this on at least a couple of earlier occasions, back in 1967 and again somewhere around 2002. Both times the water came all the way up to the windshield of the vehicle, and I made it out then, so I wasn't concerned over a couple of feet of water.

As I turned the corner out of the driveway and onto the road, however, suddenly everything disappeared. All I could see was water—the water on the road and the water spray from 140 mph winds creating a fog-like mist thicker than any fog I had ever seen, and I've seen some dense fog in my life. I stopped.

I knew the general direction I wanted to go, but if I continued, I would be driving blind. There were no waypoints—only water and mist. If I were to stray to the left, I would end up in eight feet of water. If I strayed right . . . I don't know, but still not good.

I think for the first time in my life, I panicked. I laid my phone, which was on my lap, on the console between the seats. When I did, somehow the phone dialed my son who was in Guam on a job at the time. I managed to tell him 'I'm in the water and I made a mistake—I'm going to die'. At this point, the phone went dead, and I tossed it on the dash.

I don't recall exactly what I did after that, but I was not getting anywhere fast. Suddenly, I saw one of the cypress trees I have on either side of my driveway. My yard-ornament tractor, a seventy-year-old Farmall I used to mow mesquite brush with, was nearby, as was a power pole, but I could see neither of these. All I saw was the tree. I just had to back around the right side of the tree and up the driveway to the house and relative safety.

I put the truck in reverse and backed what I thought was around the tree, but I ended up on the wrong side of the cypress. Maybe when I turned, a wave picked the rear end of my truck up and turned me around. I backed into the yard between the tree and the old tractor in water deep enough that it was now up to the door window. I was in deep shit, and I wasn't going anywhere. I quickly rolled the electric window down, so I'd have a portal through which I could escape, just before the batteries shorted out in the water.

I climbed out the door window, onto the tool-box, and held on to the ladder rack. This would be my home away from home for the next eight hours—eight hours to think how stupid I was; how I was going to die a miserable death; how I had scared my son to no end; how glad I was that Ellen, my significant other, was safe in San Antonio; and how sad it would be for her to have to identify my body.

The LED light I placed on top of my duffle bag inside the truck was still shining and giving me a little light. Otherwise, I would have been in complete darkness. Thanks to this little light, I was able to see the old tractor up against which my truck drifted. I picked a spot on the tractor and watched the water level rise slowly for the next hour; then it seemed to stop rising. The water came up a few more inches, then held steady.

Before Harvey hit, I tied the 150-gallon propane tank used to fuel the tractor to one of its wheels so it wouldn't float away. As I sat, my mind searching for a solution to my dilemma, I thought of floating with the propane tank to the highway. If the water continued to rise, that might be a decent option. There was a strong current in the water on both sides of the truck. What if I were carried into the river? What would happen then? There was also a wire fence along the highway. What if I got tangled up in that? My garden and its fencing were between me and the highway too. I could get tangled in that as well. My choices seemed dismal at best. The best option seemed to be to stay with the truck.

Finally, the water started to recede slowly, but the wind was still blowing very hard. I was not out of danger yet, but with the water now going down, if I were to sit tight, I would likely live. At that point, I got mad, first at myself for getting into this situation, but also mad in general. I yelled some lines from

Forest Gump over and over— "You call this a storm? Blow, you son-of-a-bitch, blow!" I laughed at myself, then screamed the lines again at the top of my lungs.

Daylight came, and I could finally see more than a few feet. The flow of the water around my truck was still quite strong, as was the wind. I could not traverse the current to higher ground a mere twenty feet away, though I very much wanted to do so. I kept thinking I could still die if I did something stupid again!

After six hours of lashing by the wind, rain, waves, and debris, I was one wet and tired rat. I needed to get out of the storm. The water had gone down about a foot, and if I could open the door to the truck, I could crawl inside. I busted the small center slider glass of the back window, so that I could reach inside to unlock the door. I then mashed the trash down which had accumulated between the truck and the tractor, and pulled the door open. So much trash (weeds, limbs, etc.) had gone inside the open driver's side window that there was just barely enough room for me, but I made it work. The wind was still blowing through the open window. I pulled my wet duffle bag up to the top of the pile to help shield me. It wasn't great, but it was better than outside.

By 10:30 a.m. the water was down enough that I just walked away and back to the house. My legs were like jelly, and I was sore and achy, but the relief was out of this world. I would be okay, but my cell phone was dead. I couldn't let anyone know. I found out later that my son contacted Cousin Phillip locally and he sent someone to check on me. About an hour or so later, the wind and rain had died down significantly, and Crazy Mike came by and found me alive and well. He relayed the news back to my cousin who let everyone else know I was all right.

I stayed the night with Cousin Phillip and his wife, and slept for about twelve hours, before going home. I felt much better with some sleep and a good meal, but my ordeal was not over yet. I learned first-hand what post-traumatic stress disorder (PTSD) was. Even though I'd had several brushes with death over the course of my life, I had never felt it. I was feeling it now though.

My body had been stressed, and I felt that of course, but what I didn't expect was the stress on my mind. My brain felt fuzzy—I had difficulty thinking, I couldn't hold a thought for long, my memory failed me constantly, and I seemed to be in a fog. I didn't know what was going on at first until Ellen pointed out that I had PTSD. I know now that was exactly what I had, and that it probably wouldn't last forever. I rested as much as I could, but there was an overwhelming task ahead of me—the clean-up from the storm.

To keep the clean-up task from overwhelming me, I focused only on individual projects, and when I completed them, moved on to the next in order of

Floodwaters

importance. After a week, my mind began to return to normal, or at least close for me. As I've said many times, I will never consider myself normal.

It's two weeks later, and I'm doing okay. I've juggled gas cans for the generator, which I wired directly into the breaker box on the service pole, to keep minimal electricity going; I'm keeping the septic system functional; I've installed a new water pump and tank; the house is probably cleaner than before the storm and organized again; and thanks to the power company, I've had air conditioning for 24 hours now. I feel better and life will be good again. However, it will be months before the yard is back to anything close to what it was before Harvey.

The hardest challenge has been met and dealt with, and by springtime, this will all be history as the trees that survived and Ellen and I get ready for a new year. Harvey was tough, but I am tougher. Good riddance, you son-of-a-bitch!

Aftermath: Harvey Lives On! (2017)

It's been four months since Harvey slammed into the Texas Gulf Coast. The only major thing we lost inside our home due to the hurricane was our carpet, which we were considering replacing anyway. We lost a few frozen goods in one freezer because the generator couldn't provide the needed amperage, but that was minor. I can't think of anything else of significance inside that was damaged.

Outside, the septic system was damaged, but that turned out to be minor. The water well and pump house were gone. I installed a new water pump and tank. I'll build the well-house later when time permits.

While I was installing the new water pump and tank, a brown pelican flew in and lit within a few feet of me. He didn't appear to be afraid of me, and I talked to him. He stared and nodded at my words. I went to get my phone to take a picture, and he waited until I returned. He seemed to be suffering from PTSD, just as I was. I went back to my project, and a short while later he walked over to my pond and paddled away.

Brown pelican that paid a visit

I have seen only two squirrels since the storm. They make their nests in trees, and the winds of the hurricane surely wreaked havoc with them. The good news is they won't be eating the peaches I'll get this year. Knowing that most of them died is sad though. I'd rather have them in my orchard from time to time. I can spare the fruit.

There are many more species that I don't see around either. No wrens made it here this winter. Probably the most disturbing is the lack of honey bees. In the past five months, I've seen four. They had better come out by the thousands in the spring, or we're going to have a serious pollination problem.

A few woodpeckers have come back, but they are scarce to see. A lot of predator birds are around though—Osprey, Caracara, Red-tail Hawk, Great Blue Heron, and Kingfisher. There seem to be plenty of geese and ducks. I've heard hunters shooting most mornings. These are migratory birds and were far north during Harvey.

The bulk of the outside damage should never have happened. The National Resource Conservation Service (NRCS), to which I and some of my neighbors leased most of our property for conservation purposes, was the cause of much of my damage. Part of their conservation project included removing much of the noxious brush on the property. They dug up hundreds of trees and brush and let them lay there. I was under the impression they would burn it, but they didn't. When the storm surge from Hurricane Harvey came in, it whipped all this brush into my yard.

Tons of flying and floating trees and brush ripped up three garden areas and all the fencing, and it slammed into my orchard, flattening many of the mature and bearing trees. This has been one of the devastating aspects of the aftermath. I will get some fruit next year, but it won't be nearly enough. We eat a lot of fruit.

The NRCS readily agreed the brush was their responsibility and they would clean it up. This was where the nightmare began. The brush all over the yard has been hard to take, but the clean-up has been unbearable and mentally exhausting. Let's see if you agree.

The NRCS contractors showed up two months after the storm. They did what they wanted, how they wanted to do it, and would pay no heed to my needs, desires, and warnings. As a result, they cut ruts all over my property, using equipment they should not have been using in the first place, burned brush where and when they were not authorized to do so, cut down living trees they were asked to protect, damaged my septic system and left it broken, and they did not finish the job.

Ruts in my extended front yard

Damaged fruit trees

Tales from the Riverside 127

Damaged fruit tree

Brush in front yard

A path through the brush on our driveway after Harvey

Brush in my front yard

Springtime will be here in a couple of months or so, and things will change again. We will be planting potatoes from mid-January to mid-February and much of the rest of the garden before the 1st of March. That's when we plant around here.

Things will improve, but it will not be back to normal for a very long time. Harvey was devastating to my yard, but hopefully the NRCS will repair it soon. The financial strain will linger for many years, if not for the rest of my life. The mental strain due to the NRCS contractors who removed the brush from my yard, and the damage they caused, will probably last forever.

As bad as things were and still are, I realize that I am very lucky to be alive. I will have a good garden and so will Ellen. We will get some fruit, but it won't be nearly what we had last year. The NRCS trees and brush killed more than 40 bearing-fruit trees. Others were severely damaged. It will be years before we get the orchard back to what it was before the storm. It takes time for trees to grow, and many of the trees were in the five- to ten-year range. You cannot replace these overnight.

I love my flowers too. The crepe myrtle survived the storm, but the Esperanza and Pride of Barbados took a beating. I saved seeds before the storm, so that I can replace them, and I'll be happy. One Pride of Barbados plant sprouted out from the ground after Harvey. The rest I'll plant in the spring.

Before I wrap up the aftermath of Harvey, I've gotta tell you this story.

After the storm, all the fencing was gone around my garden. The brush carried it away, and there wasn't anything but a muddy plot. I had potatoes sprouting in the house from the spring garden that needed planting. I took a batch and dug holes in the mud and planted them in five rows. Then, three weeks later, I planted another batch. I planted these, too, in mud, as it had rained again just as it regularly had since the storm. It rained again after I planted the second batch.

I planted the spuds in the mud, they grew in the mud, and just before Christmas, I dug the first batch out of the mud. I dug the second batch the day after Christmas, due to some cold weather burning the plants. These were also growing in mud. But you know what? Ellen and I got about

120 lbs. of good potatoes. I say good because they were edible, but in fact, they were quite ugly.

The potatoes grew quickly, and they became deformed. They also cracked due to the high moisture. However, they kept growing. This produced many potatoes with deep valleys all over the surface. You know what though? The potatoes are still delicious. That's what counts, isn't it?

Smell the Roses! (2018)

It's 1:00 a.m., I'm up and wide awake, and I'm writing. I was tossing and turning in bed for an hour, and my mind was churning with dreams at least an hour or two earlier. This has been a common occurrence more mornings than not the past couple of years. Most mornings, however, I generally fall back to sleep, but this morning is different. I am an author, and I have something to write about. Most of the time when this happens, I decide the stuff that pops into my head is noteworthy, but not really worth putting on paper. This time, however, I chose to write it down. The result is as follows:

The Voice in My Head
By Larry Landgraf (1-27-2018)

Each night as I lie and toss in bed,
The words and phrases charge ahead,
It happens almost every night with me,
Usually around the hours of two or three.

There's a small crevasse between my ears,
Where you'll find a small desk and chairs,
An alien shows up with his pen in hand,
Why? Well, I guess because he can.

He's working on things for my books,
Or correcting errors; that's what he cooks,
Over and over in my head, you see,
Then sharing what he writes with me.

Most nights I'll ignore him; I need my rest,
I know if I leave him alone, he'll do his best,
When I awake, if it's important I'll remember,
And if it's really good, I'll crank up the computer.

Where he came from I do not know,
But now I would never tell him to go,

He's been working so hard to help me,
This I know and can easily see.

He first showed up in two-thousand fifteen,
Having him in my head, I wasn't too keen,
But he showed me he was indeed a friend,
Helping me write my first novel way back then.

You may think I'm crazy because he's there,
But what you want to believe, I really don't care,
Because he showed up to help me for a reason,
He pointed out the path—my books of Four Seasons.

Then he must have liked what he was doing,
He's hung around and kept the words spewing,
Maybe he'll stay until I get the last volume right,
All four books side by side will be quite a sight.

He's not much better than me with typos and such,
With a good editor, it doesn't matter so much,
The story is what absolutely must be grand,
No one wants to read something boring or bland.

Whomever this little guy is, must also have his faults,
As there are nights when he takes me on walks,
Through times I remember having long past,
Looking for a story, or through me, just having a blast.

I don't know his name and haven't seen his face,
I just know he's there, us both sharing the space,
I never hear from him during the day,
I just remember what that night he had to say.

Some nights I'll get up, and we'll work together,
I don't know why, but at times this seems better,
But he's quite shy, and I seldom hear a peep,
It's almost like that he's now fallen asleep.

But I know he's there as the stories keep coming,
He's working hard and his notes he's sharing,

Fixing problems or writing totally new stuff,
That I've never seen and can't ever get enough.

He's been with me now for over three years,
The stuff we've written to share without fear,
As we know it is all good, and others will like,
The stuff we've churned out both day and night.

He also helps me market so sales will soar,
Showing me that people who read want more,
They want to know their author, you see,
Grow my brand; an introvert, I can no longer be.

So you may see me wearing my coonskin hat,
Dressed up in leather jacket; moccasins to match,
Up on display for all the world to see,
Being the author, my little friend said I must be.

I'm now getting out and am quite the extrovert,
It wasn't hard to do, and I'm enjoying the perks,
It's fun meeting and sharing myself with you,
Learn about me and my books through and through.

I've made it easy for you to know me better,
The best place to start is through Twitter,
I've done this to benefit both you and me,
Search for my handle @riverrmann and you'll see.

So the next time you pick up one of my books,
Know that the story is as good as the cover looks,
Written from the heart and compiled by the brain,
Of not only me, but the little guy who one day came.

    My life is much different than most people's. I have a country life, and though I have a lot on my plate, I take the time to smell the roses along the way. Sometimes this is not easy to do when I have so much to write. Twitter takes up a lot of time, and I still have to take care of the property. I can't neglect Ellen either.

A few blue-winged teal ducks were swimming in a rain-filled low area near the house the other day, and I took the time to watch them. Last night the frogs in my swamp were extra loud, and I stopped and listened for a few minutes. The night was especially clear, and I noticed how bright the stars were. My thought was that it would be a good night for star gazing and I recognized a few constellations.

Taking a little extra time to notice my surroundings is not an isolated event for me. This is how I live my life. When I'm writing, I try to add details about the surroundings into my characters' lives. You've read about my swamp. I hope you also felt what it's like to live here.

Epilogue

There are dozens of ways to die in a swamp. There are just as many ways to die, if not more, in the city. The difference is, at least for me, there are more reasons than I can count to live out here. Cities have their good points, Starbucks being one that I can think of off the top of my head, but I've lived short stints in cities. They are more dangerous than I think my swamp could ever get. The difference for me is that I know the swamp. I've learned how to protect myself, and though I've had some close calls, I've had just as many close calls away from home.

You take and drop me in the middle of New York City, and I'd probably be dead in a week or two. You take the city guy and drop him in the middle of my swamp, and he wouldn't last half as long. It's all about how you grew up and what you learned.

In my opinion, the most dangerous animal on this planet is man. I'll take my chances with the alligators, bees, snakes, and all the other creatures that live in my swamp.

I hope you enjoyed my stories. I certainly enjoyed sharing them with you. If you're a city dweller, then the next time you think you want to venture into the woods or maybe a swamp, remember, learn a little bit about the habitat into which you will be putting yourself. Your life depends upon it, literally.

If you don't know what you're doing, nature will kill you. It kills many who think they know what they're doing every year. That is a statistical fact. Probably the easiest and most important thing I can tell you is to watch where you're walking. Better yet, stay home and read a good book. Take a walk on the wild side with another one of my books and bypass the need for professional medical services.

My Swamp

by Larry Landgraf (1-19-2018)

The sun is shining bright,
It's warm and tropical,
Flowers are quite the sight,
The birds most comical.

A breeze rustles the leaves,
The world is serene,
Darkness comes as day recedes,
Tranquil is no longer the scene.

If it were in the city,
There would be little to say,
But for you this day it's a pity,
You're in my swamp; you'll pay.

The critters know the drill,
In day they'll not be out,
But ready for their next meal,
Under the moon, they'll prowl.

With cover of darkness, they slither,
Others buzz and sneak,
Looking for food so as not the whither,
Searching for you; the weak and meek.

They'll find you and attack,
There is nowhere for you to go,
They are the experts and have the knack,
They will survive; too bad you didn't know.

It's been this way for thousands of years,
They'll be here long after you're history,
The way the swamp endears,
The way again tonight as it will always be.

So stay out of my swamp,
Or you will surely see,
This is not a place for you to camp,
Even worse should you run into me.

About Larry Landgraf

I was born on October 21, 1948, to Lawrence Herman Landgraf and Virginia Irene (Webb) Landgraf in a Victoria, Texas, hospital. I weighed in at 9 lbs. 3-3/4 ozs., which is rather large, especially since my mother was on the thin side then. I would be a large man when I grew up. I topped out at 6 ft. 0 in. and 225 lbs., by the time I was twenty-one.

My dad was a full-blooded German, while my mother was English and Irish, with a little American Indian mixed in. Don't ask me where that came from. No one ever said, and it was never discussed, but my mother came from Oklahoma, and there were a lot of Indians around there, I hear.

I attended Victoria College for two years and graduated in 1969 with my Associates Degree. I then attended Texas A & I University in Kingsville, Texas, for two years.

I majored in mathematics and attained minors in chemistry, biology, and history. I dropped out just shy of attaining a degree when advanced calculus went over my head and I could not advance without it.

While I learned a lot, what I learned most was that I didn't want to be cooped up in an office or classroom the rest of my life. For this reason, I moved home to Tivoli and undertook my new career as a commercial fisherman. This is where my education really began—learning things often by failing in the *School of Hard Knocks*.

I married while attending college in Kingsville and returned to Tivoli in 1971 with my bride. I know now that I was way too young to be getting married, but shit happens. I moved the following year to where I currently reside on the bank of the Guadalupe River in Refugio County, Texas.

When my commercial fishing career played out in 1989, I undertook a career as a general contractor in 1990. I worked primarily as a roofing contractor much of this period and sold products manufactured by a coatings company in Fort Worth, Texas.

I started out slow, as would be expected by a newbie. I worked very hard, mostly alone, and hired a few helpers after the first couple of years when I had learned enough to procure more work. I ended up with many awards from this manufacturing company and sold well over a million dollars of their products. If you have read all the stories in this book, you already know how and why this career ended.

I divorced in 2008, a marriage which produced three children. I currently reside in the home I built with my own two hands with my beloved Ellen, whom I met in 2009. We plan to grow old together and see no end to this relationship. If you want to know me better, the best place is my autobiography, *How to Be a Smart SOB Like Me*.

Fresh Ink Group

Publishing
Free Memberships
Free-Story Newsletter
Writing Contests

🖉

Books
Ebooks

🖉

Authors
Editors
Artists
Professionals
Publishing Services
Publisher Resources

🖉

Members' Websites
Members' Blogs
Social Media

FreshInkGroup.com
Email: info@FreshInkGroup.com
Twitter: @FreshInkGroup
Google+: Fresh Ink Group
Facebook.com/FreshInkGroup
LinkedIn: Fresh Ink Group

Also by Larry Landgraf

Self-help/Autobiography

How to Be a Smart SOB Like Me

The Four Seasons Series

Into Autumn - A Story of Survival
Into Spring - The Next Generation
Into Winter - The Armed Invasion
Into Summer - Dawn of a New Age (Summer 2018)

A Tempest in Texas (screenplay) based on *Into Autumn*

Watch for more screenplays in development.

Larry's Books are available at all book retailers worldwide, including Barnes & Noble, Amazon, GooglePlay, iBooks, iTunes, Kobo, Overdrive, and more.

Larry's Author Site

www.IntoAutumn.com

Larry's Books on Amazon

https://www.amazon.com/s/ref=nb_sb_ss_c_2_14?url=search-alias%3Dstripbooks&field-keywords=larry+landgraf&sprefix=Larry+Landgraf%2Caps%2C806&crid=2SC9416D5H8CY

Larry's Amazon Author Central

https://www.amazon.com/Larry-Landgraf/e/B00NS3YRLO/ref=sr_tc_2_0?qid=1510272488&sr=1-2-ent

Larry's YouTube Channel

https://www.youtube.com/playlist?list=PLHAl2COVDWFIpDB_B8AkoRp3iiaXaKCaC

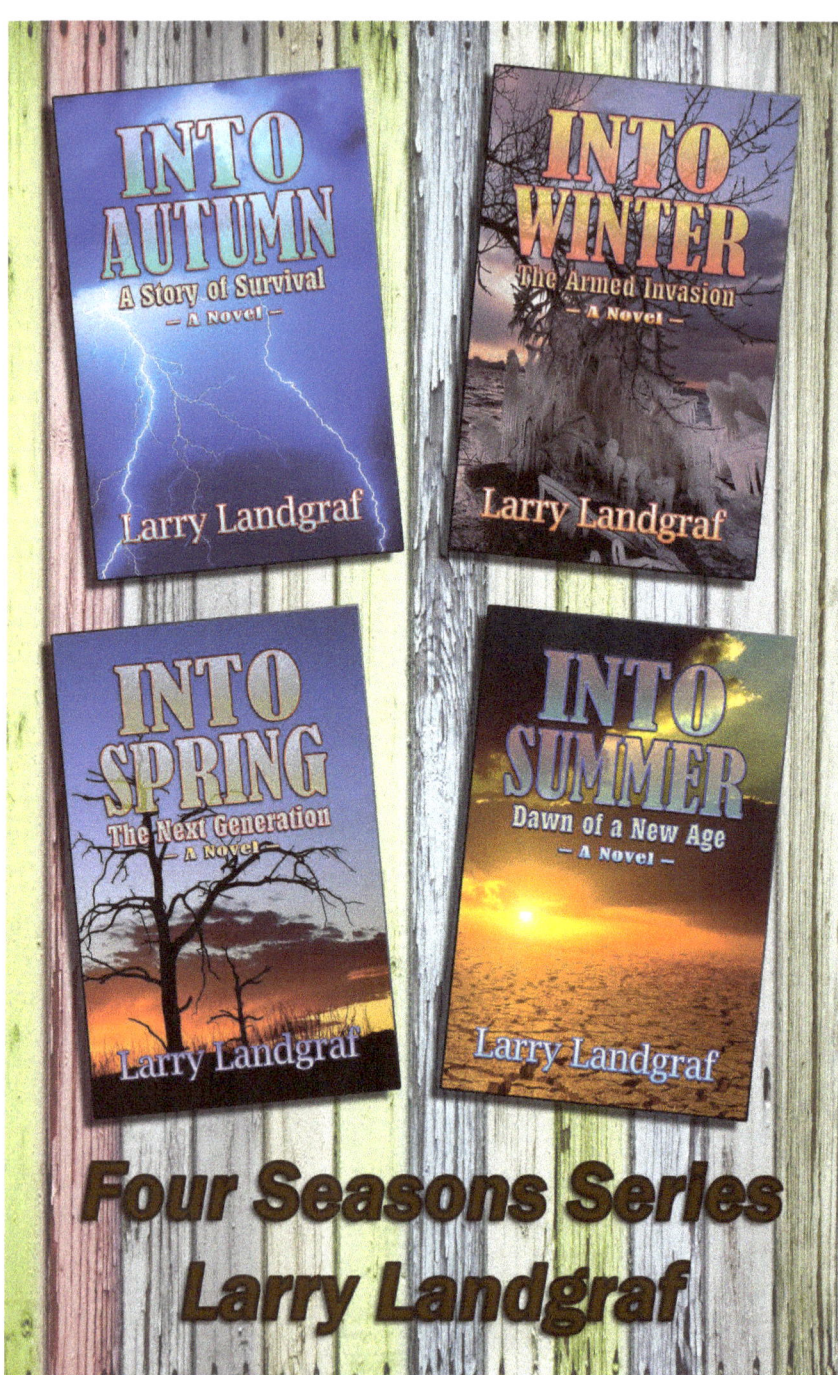

Work, money, food, relationships, life in general—these are the everyday struggles for billions crowded into our challenging world. Larry Landgraf tells us his story and the many lessons he's learned for finding extraordinary happiness. *How to Be a Smart SOB Like Me* is a stark but heartfelt examination of a life well-lived. You might like him, and you might not, but you can't help but learn ways you, too, can achieve your best.

www.ingramcontent.com/pod-product-compliance
Lightning Source LLC
Chambersburg PA
CBHW041957080526
44588CB00021B/2776